HAGERMAN

Tony Reeve

VIOLET
CROWN
Publishers

Austin, Texas

PUBLISHER'S NOTE

Copyright © 2014 by Tony Reeve
Cover design: Anna K. Sargent
Interior design: Tosh McIntosh
Front Cover Photo: Paid for commercial rights permission from Fotosearch.com

Printed and published in the United States of America
Violet Crown Publishers
ISBN-13: 978-1-938749-25-4
ISBN-10: 1938749251

To all past, present, and future cadets of
New Mexico Military Institute

★★★★★ "A must read for football fans, but those like myself who know little about the game will find this a unique and heartwarming coming-of-age story."

—Lara Reznik, bestselling Amazon Author

HAGERMAN

CHAPTER ONE

I grew up in Premium, Texas, a small town where everyone knows everyone, and football is not a sport but a religion. The first game I started in at Premium High, I threw for over three hundred yards, rushed for another hundred, and put up five touchdowns, three through the air and running two in.

From that day on, the entire town knew who I was and treated me like a king. Everywhere I went people would kiss my ass, and when that happens, your arrogance grows to mammoth proportions. I'm the first to admit that my ego grew as big as the football field after three years of this treatment.

Even though my talents on the field were far superior to all my teammates, and people treated me better than everyone else, I took it in stride as Rocky Montoya's deserved role in life.

At home, life was quite different. The night of my junior year State Championship began with a typical unpleasant dinner with my mother. My father had left us when I was too young to remember, so it was just the two of us in the kitchen of the small triplex apartment.

I walked inside the house and smelled the aroma of the leftover Kentucky Fried chicken she had just reheated from the other night. My mother wasn't much of a cook and we ate fast food more often than not.

"How was your day?" I tossed my books on the table.

"Shitty as always," she said. "Mr. Blake thinks because I work in his crappy pizza joint, he has a right to pinch my ass. Next time he tries it, I'll cut off his fingers."

I sat down at the table and she served the chicken on some paper plates. "Sorry your day was so bad." I wanted to sound sympathetic but my heart wasn't in it. When your mother has a crappy day every day and doesn't bother to ask you about your day, it's hard to really care. I picked at the petrified chicken on my plate. She'd overheated it in the microwave as usual. "Are you coming to the game tonight?"

She furrowed her forehead. "What game?"

"It's the State Championship. Remember, I've been talking about it for weeks." I tried to keep my tone calm but I felt like I would explode. How could my mother forget about the State Championship? Here I was the starting quarterback at Premium High School and everyone in town thought I walked on water. But to her, I was just an annoyance. A stupid kid she had to support whose old man took off the first chance he got.

She took her plate and placed it in the sink. "You know, Rocky, my life doesn't revolve around you. I have a date tonight with a nice gentleman who came into the restaurant."

My voice croaked. "I guess that's more important than watching your son play in the State Championship game."

Next thing I knew she slapped me across the face. "Don't you be sassy with me, young man. You remind me —"

"Of my father?" My face stung more from the shock than the slap.

"Don't bring his name up to me."

"Well, maybe, it's about time you told me what happened to him."

She glared at me with daggers in her eyes. "He just upped and quit on us, boy. And I expect once you get some fancy scholarship to college, you'll up and quit on me too."

I couldn't wait to leave the house and as soon as I'd finished the dried out chicken breast, I packed my gear, charged from the house and headed to the locker room at school. The game started at seven. The stands were packed with everyone from the high school and parents of the team. The cheerleaders stood by the goal in their short skirts and tight sweaters. They incited the crowd with our Premium High School cheer led by my drop dead gorgeous girlfriend, Ashley. She blew me a kiss and I fantasized about our private celebration later after the keggers.

Coach Jackson took me aside. "Now, Rocky, remember as quarterback you're the leader of this team and you gotta direct and inspire the other guys." Coach knew leadership was my biggest weakness but it was going to be needed from me to win the championship tonight. I nodded.

Throughout the game, I played great but the opposition played just as skillful a game, and had the lead as we headed into the last minute. Just down by two points, all I needed to do was drive my team down seventy yards to get our special teams into field goal range. A field goal would win the game for us, and it was crucial I give our kicker an opportunity to win us our first State Championship.

The drive started out fine with a few quick passes and a screen that gave us some decent yards before we called our last timeout to stop the game. We were at our forty-five yard line and needed at least twenty-five more yards to give our kicker a shot to put the game away.

The first play I lined up under center and snapped the ball. Two seconds later, I was hit from behind, taking the sack. The clock continued to run under a minute and I felt that heavy feeling in the pit of my stomach. My hands were wet with sweat and my breathing got heavier with each passing second. The lights over the football field were brighter than usual and a thousand things raced through my mind. Then I had a thought that would lead to my undoing and ultimate failure. The thought was simple: I can't do this.

The crowd was on its feet and although I knew they were all yelling as loud as they could, there was nothing but silence for me. Coming to the line I could feel my heart pumping in full throttle. I smelled nothing but the sweat coming from everyone around me. It was an uncomfortable feeling in a moment where I needed comfort.

I tried to gather the offense and call out a play at the line of scrimmage, but there was no conviction in my voice, no confidence in my body language. Before I knew it, the ball had been snapped into my hands and I dropped back three steps and stood tall in the pocket. I had done this a thousand times before but this was different. Unlike every other play where things move a lot slower allowing me to read coverage with ease, things progressed at what seemed like a thousand miles per hour. I could not read the coverage that the secondary and linebackers were lined up in.

A few seconds in the pocket, I had held onto the ball too long and I needed to get it out of my hands. I forced the ball into a small window where I thought my wide receiver was open. That window rapidly closed, forcing an incomplete pass.

The clock had slipped to under thirty seconds, and we were now thirty yards from where we needed to be because of the five-yard sack I took on first down. I also had to take into consideration the down and the distance. I needed those fifteen yards to get the first down to give us maybe an extra play or two. I stepped to the line of scrimmage, third and fifteen yards to the first down at midfield, the game in my hands. The pressure was getting to me now, as time was running out to win the State Championship.

Everyone was counting on me to make the play to bring the title home. Ashley's long blonde hair blew in the wind, her full lips parted as she and the crowd waited for me to make my move. As I stood behind my center barking orders to my lineman and receivers, I had this terrible urge to disappear. I wanted to be anywhere but there.

Something about pressure defines a person. They either rise to the occasion and do what is needed to get the job done, or they fold. I wish I could tell you that I made a miraculous play to win the game, but that would be a lie. I folded.

The ball was snapped into my hands and I dropped back five steps this time, to give my receivers another half second to get open, but it did not matter. The defensive line broke through the line. I sidestepped allowing for my left guard to block a pressuring defensive lineman away from me.

The second defensive tackle managed to get his left hand onto my left shoulder pad causing me to lose balance.

I shoved him off but because he succeeded in slowing me down I was out of sync with my wide receiver. Their left defensive end and blitzing middle linebacker had shrugged off my lineman and were about to sack me. I rolled out of the pocket to buy some more time and attempt a good pass. This essentially transformed me into the likes of a backyard football player with their secondary and my receivers.

My tight end had found a gap in the secondary. He was running parallel with me about twenty yards down field. I took the ball and side-armed it like a rocket to my tight end.

The ball was dead on target. Perhaps if the ball had been thrown a split second earlier, it would have hit my guy dead between the numbers, but I'd been completely baited into throwing that football. The strong safety also ran parallel with my tight end and me, creating the gap separation. I assumed my guy was open. When I wound up and threw the football, he planted his left foot into the ground and cut back into the throwing lane allowing for an easy interception. This ended the game and my reputation as a hero in Premium, Texas.

I immediately raced into the locker room knowing that everyone was going to blame me. That's what comes with being a football hero. When you fuck up, you're hated. I blew it and caused us to lose the championship! As I got dressed, no one looked at me. Some seniors were near their dressing areas crying, others had stunned looks on their faces. A couple of the guys glared at me with angry eyes. As I finished getting dressed one of the lineman pointed at me and said, "What a retard."

I flew back in his direction. "Fuck you, fat boy, I'd like to see you do better."

He stood. "You walk around like your shit don't stink when all you really are is a clown."

I lunged at him but the rest of the team quickly restrained me and separated us.

I shoved the guys off of me, threw my bag on my shoulder, and bolted from the room. Everyone scowled at me like I was a piranha. Not one stopped me to tell me that it was a team game, and we had lost it as a team. No, that's not how it worked. In everyone's eyes, I personally lost the game.

Ashley, in all her blonde perfection stood in the parking lot laughing with a couple of her cheerleader girlfriends.

"Ashley," I yelled.

She ignored me.

"Ashley," I shouted again.

But she just sniffed at me like I was a skunk. Then she got into her friend Heather's SUV.

I peeled out of the parking lot in my truck and drove to my house. I knew my mother was out on her date and wouldn't be home anytime soon. So I entered the kitchen and reached in the back of a cabinet where my mother hid her liquor. There, I retrieved a bottle of whisky that was about half empty.

Racing from the house with the bottle in hand, I jumped into my truck, and sped off. I didn't know where I was going, since I figured everyone I knew hated me. The thought of Ashley hurt the most.

I turned on the radio in time to hear our local Premium station's commentary on the game. The radio host spoke in a despondent voice. "All we can really do at this point is wonder what was going through Montoya's head when he released the ball. The boy let us all down in our championship game. You got to really feel for the other young men who put in all the hard work throughout the season just to have their dreams and hopes shattered by a boneheaded play. We are taking your calls, 972-RADIO …"

Tears now on my cheeks, I shut the radio off. After driving around aimlessly, I parked in a dirt field just outside of town. The only thing I could hear was the liquid as I chugged down the whiskey.

A lot went through my mind that night, and none of it had to do with football. It's funny how you can easily decipher your problems when you are at your lowest point. I thought about how screwed up the situation was that I lived in, and how even more messed up of a person I'd become. There was nothing for me in Premium without football. I had one parent who'd deserted me and couldn't give a shit about what was happening in my life, and another who made me feel like I was nothing but a burden. I now knew the truth about Ashley. The only reason she or anyone else in this town hung out with me was for what I did for the football team. My girlfriend and the rest of my "so called friends" could care less about me now that I'd screwed up, and at my darkest hour.

Soon my emotions changed to anger as I thought of all the other kids on the team at home right now being consoled by their fathers. I kept asking myself, why couldn't I have that?

As these thoughts went back and forth in my head, the bottle went dry. I glanced at the dashboard clock. 3:30 am. I wasn't the least bit tired, just angry and sad all at the same time.

I was about to pull back onto the highway, when I heard a knock on my window. A bright light was shining directly into my face. Behind the light stood a state police officer. My anger did not convert into fear for being in possession of alcohol, but instead it doubled. I kept thinking to myself, "Why can't I get a break? Why can't people just leave me alone?"

The cop moved closer, tapping my window to signal me to

roll it down. Then he stared at me for a second. "What are you doing out here, this time of night, son?"

I hesitated for a moment before opening my mouth. "Just wanted to get away for a little, officer."

The officer looked at me as if he knew I was hiding something. "You been doing any drinking tonight?"

"Ah, not really."

"Step out of the vehicle, young man." It was all over now.

"Stand right there and don't move. I need to check out the cab of your truck." As he headed toward the passenger door, I wound up my fist and hit him in the back, knocking him to the ground.

Then I really panicked. Sweat ran down my face and neck as I flew inside my truck, cranked the engine, and sped off. Seconds later his red-and-blue lights were flashing in my review mirror. I didn't have a plan and felt so beaten down from life. I just didn't care anymore. There was no fear rushing through me. I wanted one thing, and stupid as this sounds, I wanted the cops to earn me.

Soon, I noticed another pair of red-and-blue lights flashing behind me as I raced down a deserted road. I pushed down on the gas pedal and planned my next move. I was driving through alleys, and turning off on different roads. Before long a third pair of lights joined the other two squad cars and I thought how much I was enjoying this. I know now it was the alcohol doing the thinking for me.

Less than ten minutes had passed before my first and only plan came to me. Stupid idiot that I was, I thought that I could outrun the officers' vehicles if I were on dirt terrain. So I turned onto a road that ran parallel to the open desert. The three cops raced behind me and no matter how hard I accelerated I couldn't gain any separation from them. Then, I noticed an opening in the fences that separated the road from the dirt. I planned to make a hard left, but knew I was going too fast to make the turn without flipping the truck.

What happened next is only what I have heard from others because I don't remember any of it. I've been told that when I lifted off the gas pedal and turned left, one of the squad cars accelerated into the back end of my truck. This caused enough of an imbalance to my truck that it actually flipped over several times into the desert before coming to a rest. The doctors said it was a miracle I did not sustain any more injuries than the concussion and multiple lacerations over my face and shoulders.

As you can imagine, I was in pretty deep shit. After a few days, I left the hospital.

"Get your crap and get the hell out my house!" my mother shouted at me when I saw her for the first time as I entered the doorway. "You're going to move in with your Aunt Patty. And you're a lucky son-of-a-bitch she's willing to have you. Otherwise, you'd be alone on the street."

I swallowed hard trying to hold back tears. "Mom, please, don't make me go live with that religious fanatic," I pleaded. I was sure the only reason my aunt Patty, a born-again Christian, wanted me was so she could "save" me. She probably got some credit with her church. Even though she was Mom's sister, they barely spoke. She'd always put my mother's lifestyle down. Told her she lived in sin and needed for us both to find Jesus.

"Maybe a dose of religion would do you good, boy," my mother said.

"I promise to be better. I won't be stupid anymore," I said. "Just let me stay here and live with you, Mom. You've told me on more than one occasion Aunt Patty is nuts."

"I'm done with you, boy. You are a worthless piece of shit like your father." She wagged her finger at me. "Want to be a bad ass? Want to walk around like the rules don't apply to you? You do that out of my sight and out of my life."

It didn't take a genius to realize that no convincing would change my mother's mind. I headed to my room, gathered some clothes into my gym bag and left the house, slamming the door behind me.

Premium High School had expelled me and all of the college recruits were long gone. All that was left for me was to wait to see what the judge was going to do to me.

I sat in the courtroom dressed in a ratty grey suit that was too tight and smelled like mothballs. My aunt had dug it out of the back of a closet. It had belonged to Uncle Phil who had died of cancer a few years back.

I peered down at black loafers, also a remnant from my dead uncle. I was a scared boy, too afraid to even look at the judge as she stared right through me.

"So, the hotshot quarterback from Premium High School thinks he is a celebrity and can do what he wants?" the judge said to me with piercing blue-grey eyes. She had thin brown eyebrows that arched as she spoke.

I bit my lip. "I was scared, Judge."

She shook her head. "You do realize, your punishment would have been a lot easier if you would have let the officer just do his job and not touched him."

"I realize, Your Honor, and I am very sorry for my actions."

"Look at you," she said. "You wouldn't last one day in a jail cell with real criminals. You're just a boy. A scared little boy. You need someone to teach you to be a man. I don't think jail can teach you that."

"Please Your Honor, I will do anything to keep from going to jail."

She scratched her head and the room was silent for a long few minutes. Finally, she looked me square in the eyes. "Well, there is another option. You won't like it though, I can guarantee that."

CHAPTER TWO

Hagerman Military Institute is where the judge sentenced me to go. I had no idea what the place was but I figured what could possibly be worse than jail? I would later learn that Hagerman Military Institute was a military school in southern New Mexico and it would be my home for the next year.

If you've ever been in Texas in the summer, you'll understand the torture of the long drive in Aunt Patty's old Ford station wagon that was not equipped with air conditioning. If you haven't had the pleasure of hanging out in the best BBQ state in America where everything sizzles in ninety-nine degree heat for days on end, then you now get the picture.

All that lay ahead of my aunt and me was the endless stretches of flat, brown dirt and white cotton as we made the three-hour drive to Hagerman Military Institute. Staring off into the distance with nothing to occupy my thoughts but the vast desert around us, I found myself less concerned with the challenge of the new school, than the sweltering heat on this summer afternoon. I imagined how bad the next few weeks were going be, playing military in this heat every day.

Three hours passed without a word between us. Aunt Patty tried her religious crap on me for the first fifty miles, but had figured out that I wasn't about to be "born again." The smell of her cheap perfume and body odor filled the car. I felt nauseated staring at the big mole above her lip with a hair that begged to be plucked. I stared anyway out of boredom. I figured she hated me as much as my mother, but thought that it was simply her Christian duty to drive me all the way to Roswell, New Mexico.

It didn't matter to me, I had never liked her much either. She was nosey and overbearing so I was both surprised and grateful for the three-hour silence.

As I watched the road signs that we were passing, I would scan the horizon for Roswell. The declining miles on the signs told us how far we appeared to be diminishing at an incredibly slow pace. I craved to arrive at our destination and get this whole ordeal over with. My long legs crumpled up in the front seat, and my suitcases sat perched in the back.

When we came within a hundred miles of Roswell, we passed through a small town that was so insignificant I never caught the name of it. The buildings reminded me of the latest horror film, The Texas Chainsaw Massacre. It was such an eerie feeling driving less than twenty-five miles per hour through it. There wasn't a single soul walking around. It felt as if we were crawling through a ghost town. Paint flaked and peeled on the side of the cafe that reflected the mood and atmosphere. Back on the highway, past the desolate town, I felt a sense of normalcy again and breathed a sigh of relief to see the wide-open desert once more.

After what seemed like an eternity, I noticed that we were within ten miles of the outer city limits leading to Roswell.

The dirt turned into grass on the outskirts of the town, where farmers were growing their crops. The sun went down in the west so the lights from building were still not yet visible, but I began to see the outlines of where two buildings stood.

Upon entering the city, it strangely reminded me of Premium. Small billboards appeared on the side of the road advertising hotels or restaurants. Passing under a small bridge, buildings sprouted up on the side of the highway and a sign said, "Welcome to Roswell." Much to the sign's contradiction, I did not feel welcome there.

Aunt Patty drove more slowly and there was a very distinct smell of cow shit that would soon become the defining feature of the city of Roswell for me. Beyond those buildings, standing on the side of the road were herds of grazing cattle.

Eventually, I noticed a sign that said that Hagerman was less than a mile away. I had no idea what the school even looked like. There were a few billboards with restaurant advertisements and an occasional hotel, but no more Hagerman signs. According to our map, the school would appear on the right hand side of the road. As we passed a Domino's Pizza place I sat back in my seat.

And then it appeared in front us, a sight that I would never forget. I was overwhelmed by how I felt. The sudden presence of this strangely impressive campus, with its long fields and large buildings, had been designed to imitate a castle. The tall brown brick structures displayed flags along the top, some waved the school logo, others the New Mexico flag, and of course, the American flag.

We passed one building that extended at least a quarter of the campus. It stood three stories tall. I tried to look through the windows to see what was inside. All I could see was two bunk beds, so naturally I assumed that this building was the dorms. As we drove under the bridge that connected the campus to baseball fields and a football stadium across the street, I tried to get a glimpse of the turf I loved so much. From what I could see, the stadium was twice as big as the one I played in at Premium. As my eyes stretched beyond the sports fields, I saw a very impressive building, again castle-like, that displayed an intricate clock tower.

Driving along, we managed to catch every green light and what only took seconds seemed like an eternity for me. For the first time in three hours, I finally spoke to my aunt. "What's the plan?"

"We need to check into the hotel now and then there is some sort of assembly for the incoming students," she said.

"Do you know where that is?"

"I know just as much about this place as you do," she answered in a sarcastic tone. "Lets check into the hotel then we can head over to Hagerman and ask someone where we need to go. I'm sure there are a lot of incoming kids, in the same boat." I was sure she wanted to ditch me as soon as possible.

We did as she dictated and checked into a hotel not too far from campus and then headed back to find out where the assembly was taking place. As we ambled through the campus, I was affected by what I saw. Not only from an outward appearance, the buildings within the campus all had an imposing castle look to them. We walked past the church, which I must have missed when we drove in, and noticed it was now a short distance from the incredible clock tower I'd seen earlier.

Heading down a white path surrounded by bricks, I wondered about the significance of the white pavement when I noticed a very tall guy dressed in a military uniform. He wore a tan long-sleeved shirt with his tie tucked into and through his third button. There were medals and small ribbons covering his left chest, and I counted five stripes over his shoulders. He wore black shoes, green pants, a green hat shaped like a sailor's cap and a shiny gold belt. The belt displayed Hagerman's name over a bronco emblem.

The guy paced back-and-forth on a narrow black mat about ten yards long and one yard wide, with a rifle over his right shoulder. There was a flame that was encased in the middle of a brick structure and I could tell he was guarding something important.

We entered through a pass into the barracks, which was clearly the dorm area. Three stories high, each dorm section was divided by company name. I knew the companies because of all of the war movies I'd watched. The names Alpha, Bravo, and Charlie were the giveaway for me. Beyond the barracks was an office where two guys in uniform were sitting. Both seemed like they were waiting to assist people like us trying to find the assembly.

My aunt spoke to one of the cadets. "Excuse me, can you tell us where the assembly for new students is?"

The young guy with two bars on his right chest responded with a bright smile. "Yes, ma'am, the assembly will be taking place in Bronco Hall. Walk through the dorms, or what we here call 'the box'. Then turn right and walk until you see two cadets in uniforms like ours. They will point you to the assembly hall you're looking for."

"Thank you," she said.

"My pleasure, ma'am."

Once through the gap we saw what the guy called "the box," a field of grass dissected by a maze of pavement at its center. We approached the building where people entered dressed in normal clothing. I assumed they were parents and incoming students. Inside, there were probably 1,500 seats all pointing to a stage with a microphone stand. There were two levels of seats. The bottom level was for families. On the second level, there were hundreds of people in uniform.

My aunt and I took our seats near the front of the auditorium, close to the aisle. I slouched a bit in my chair, a thousand different things running through my mind. Though I was impressed with the campus, and even the guides in uniform, there was no part of me that wanted to be there. I kept thinking of the freedom I was about to sacrifice, and how stupid I was for screwing up my life all those months ago. I contemplated my actions that night and what led me to drink, hit a cop and run from three separate squad cars.

Those rows of uniforms on the second deck behind me were a constant reminder that this was my punishment for being an idiot. But really what had me most nervous was the fact that I didn't know if I'd ever touch a football field again. Football is all I did well and I was now unsure how to go about my daily life without it. My actions that night may have cost me that luxury.

As all of these things raced through my mind, the doors to the auditorium closed. The room was illuminated and the noise within it dwindled to a whisper. My eyes turned to the microphone but I had no idea what to expect.

At that moment, a tall bald man entered the stage near the right curtain. When he walked in everyone in uniform rapidly stood. His pace was brisk and he took every step with pride. His formal uniform was unlike any other on campus, with numerous medals and a single star located on both shoulders signifying his rank of general. Several other medals decorated his lower left chest, but what stood out the most to me were his shoes. They were black like everyone else's but they shined so bright you could see your reflection in them.

As the man reached for the microphone, he had a smirk on his face. He smiled up at those on the second level and then looked down at the rest of us. "Welcome parents and all future cadets." I had no idea what he meant by cadets. Hell I did not even know what a cadet was.

"My name is Brigadier General Castle. To all of you new students from this day forward, while you attend Hagerman Military Institute, you will be a cadet. Today is the day that you begin a remarkable journey that will transform you from young boys and girls to men and women in society. I am not going to lie. Many of you are not going to successfully complete this journey and only those who want to be here the most will succeed. Sitting behind you are those new and old cadets. New cadets are those who have attended Hagerman for more than a year but less than two years. Old cadets are those who have attended this institute for two or more years. You can distinguish the two by the red bars above their name-tag. One bar represents a new cadet, and two bars signify for an old cadet."

He continued. "Ultimately, the goal of each and everyone one of you is to become a new cadet but you will have to earn it. I would like to congratulate all of you on taking the first step in the amazing journey that lies before you."

As soon as General Castle concluded his speech he took one step backwards, and then another man walked onto the stage. He didn't look much older than me. He too walked at a brisk pace, but wore a much different uniform than the General. He wore the cadet short sleeve plaid shirt with just a nametag, two red bars, and three diamonds over his shoulder boards, signifying his rank.

He walked from the right side of the stage looking straight ahead. When he reached the General, he came to a complete stop, still looking straight ahead. His feet were at first standing together, and then he slid one to face the general the other following, creating a quick and smooth right face maneuver, allowing him to look into the General's eyes.

As soon as this happened, every cadet in the second deck stood up again. After a moment's pause, the young man on stage began to lift his right hand, up to his eyebrow in what looked like a salute. The General returned the salute and then marched off stage as each of their right hands reached their sides. The cadet then turned around in a similar maneuver as he did to face the General. I have to admit it was kind of cool.

"Sit," the cadet shouted into the microphone. His eyes fixed on the cadets in the second deck, "As General Castle said before, welcome parents and all incoming students. My name is Alex Adams, or Colonel Adams to every cadet and incoming cadet in this auditorium. I have attended Hagerman now for six years, from my freshman year of high school to this year. I am a sophomore in Hagerman's Junior College."

I did not know that Hagerman was a junior college as well.

I began to realize that the junior college cadets were in charge. This fact made me nervous.

Sitting still, I noticed an incoming cadet in the third row who was talking to his friend. He looked like a slouch and someone who did want to be there. I ignored him and continued to listen.

Colonel Adams continued, "I can honestly say that coming to this fine institution was the best decision I have ever made, and I remember when it was me in a chair where you incoming cadets are sitting now. I am not going feed you lies about this place, it's tough. It will probably be the toughest thing you have ever faced to date but I promise you that if you give this place everything you have, you will come out a successful person in the end. Every cadet sitting behind you can attest to this."

The talking from the slouch in the third row continued to grow louder to a point where it was distracting. General Castle walked back on stage, halfway until he stopped in front of the kid talking. He stood there staring at him while the slouch continued to talk not noticing that the General had come on stage and was looking at him.

"Excuse me, are we interrupting your conversation, young man?" The General said with a sour look on his face.

The cadet closed his mouth and gazed at the Commandant on stage. There was an awkward silence, with no one not really knowing what was going to happen next.

General Castle continued, "You know what, I can already tell you aren't what we are looking for. You and your friend can remove yourselves from this auditorium."

Again there was on award silence with a couple snickers from the second row cadets.

"Go on," General Castle said. "Leave. You're done at Hagerman."

The two guys stood from their seats, still stunned. One of them spoke in a choked voice. "Sir, I'm really sorry, I didn't realize—"

"That you showed rude, disrespectful behavior? We don't have time for that here at Hagerman. Now head out the door, son. I wish you luck in your life. But it won't be at this Institute."

The kid and his friend walked to the back of the auditorium and left through an exit. When the door closed behind them, the Commandant left the stage and the RC continued on with his speech.

While the RC was speaking, everyone was still stunned at what had just happened, including me. That guy didn't deserve the boot, but man if something as simple as talking during a speech could get me kicked out I was going to have to be that much more careful.

I sat straight ahead and listened to the RC. "Now as a RAT, for the first three weeks, this will be your every day uniform," he said, as a different cadet walked onto stage displaying the RAT uniform, a red T-Shirt, displaying the Hagerman symbol, black shorts, a red hat, and the ugliest red and black striped socks, pulled all the way up to the cadet's knees. "When you become a new cadet, you will be allowed to wear the uniform without the socks and hat. It is kind of a privilege you will have to earn. The next uniform is what you will wear most of your time at Hagerman. It is called the Class C uniform. This uniform is your every day uniform, post the twenty-one day period unless you are told otherwise, because of a special event."

As soon as this was said, another cadet walked onto the

stage wearing the Class C uniform. It was the same uniform that the RC wore and the uniform each cadet in the second deck had on. It was the short-sleeved uniform, except there was no rank like the other uniforms that each cadet was wearing. On the end of each color the cadet displayed a pair of shinning brass.

"As RATs, you will have to wear the uniform without rank, when you have reached the status of new cadet you will be promoted to private, our lowest rank in the core. From then on you will have opportunities to be promoted within the core of cadets."

At this point in his speech, I began to space out what was being said. I did not want to be there. I thought about how at this time in prior years, I would be in the middle of summer practices, getting ready for football season. This included a daily workout in the gym working my ass off to get my body ready for the upcoming season. I'd be spending my nights sneaking into Ashley's bedroom window after her parents were asleep.

It felt like it had been forever since I last stepped foot in a gym. Then it hit me that a football team at Hagerman would be amazing. The summer was nearly over, and we were here three weeks early to get ready for this military training crap. I even heard from the RC later in his speech that not all of the cadets had arrived, and that those sitting in the second deck behind us had elected to return early to help train us, and gain recognition in the core in order to become promoted.

Could I even play football for this school? How hard was it to get a starting position here? I had never even heard of this program, since it was in New Mexico and I came from Texas. I needed to find out when practice started, and try and get into the coaches office as soon as possible to see if I was eligible to play. If I was, I would kick ass in the game like I always had before. Even if there was a player who had been starting for years, I knew I'd be better, so it was not even a concern of mine that I would earn a starting position after the coaches saw what I had to offer.

The RC wrapped up his speech. He finished with some closing words, wishing us luck. A part of me was not buying what was going on around me with all of the cadets constantly smiling and being courteous. I felt it was all for show and after the parents left, shit was going to get really hard, really fast. While these thoughts ran through my head, the General appeared again on the stage in front of the RC, who saluted him and made a quick left face and walked off stage. The General paused and, looking out at us, explained how the matriculation process for tomorrow was going to work.

"Incoming cadets are to arrive at 0800 tomorrow morning. When you arrive we will tell you where to go from there. Parents, we will be collecting cell phones and computers upon your cadet's arrival so you probably should say your goodbyes before you drop them off. Good luck to all of you."

When General Castle concluded there was a round of applause from the audience and everyone moved for the doors and we headed back to the hotel. My aunt undressed in the bathroom and came out in a ratty flannel robe. She left her teeth in a jar on the sink. "Well, I hope this place teaches you how to be a decent human. Your mother clearly did a pretty horrible job." She eventually fell asleep after carrying on about how I needed to grow up. How it wouldn't hurt me to attend a few of the local church services.

She left her purse open on the dresser. Part of me thought about taking a few bills from her wallet and head to the nearest Greyhound to go anywhere but here. It would be so simple, so easy and no one would know where I was for hours.

CHAPTER THREE

The next morning the sun rose, creating a tranquil feeling within me. I woke up an hour early to take a shower and go down to the lobby to get some complimentary breakfast. Then I ventured outside and placed my luggage into the back of my aunt's car, simultaneously staring at Hagerman's campus across the street. I spotted several vehicles turning into the campus parking lot and assumed the majority of them were RATs like myself. It still hadn't yet hit me what I was about to get myself into.

I'd just finished packing everything into the car, when my aunt came out of the front door of the hotel, with her bag in hand. She pushed her luggage in the back seat, got into the car, and started the ignition. We drove across the street following several cars hoping they knew where to start the matriculation process. We pulled onto the street, where we'd walked down from the box to the auditorium the night before. My aunt pulled onto the side of the road, close to one of the entrances of the box. She then turned the car off. "I'm going to leave you now. Do you need anything else from me?"

I looked down at my worn tennis shoes, "No, I'm fine."

"I can, ah, help you take your bags to where you need to go."

"No, I can handle it from here on. Thank you for the ride, and everything, I really do appreciate it."

She almost smiled. "Don't mention it. Good luck here."

I stepped out of the car and grabbed my suitcases out of the back of her trunk, then headed towards the entrance of the box.

My aunt stepped on the gas and sped off like a bat out of hell. I doubted I'd ever see her in Roswell again. As much as I disliked the woman, a part of me felt sad that she was all the family I had and she couldn't get out of Dodge quick enough. I felt jealous when I looked at all the other kids with their families here to see them off. A number of the parents had tears in their eyes as they said their goodbyes to their sons and daughters. Even some of the kids looked really sad. Except me. No one gave a shit regarding me. I had no one.

At the same time, I made up my mind that I'd never, let anyone find out the real reason I was here. If they knew what I'd done, then they would target me like an animal, and make my life a living hell. My plan was to just blend in. Get this year over with and move on with my life.

As I walked up to the entrance, I saw several cadets standing at the front, organizing people, telling them where to go. Nearly all of the cadets had at least three stripes on their shoulders, but I still couldn't tell the difference in rank. I walked up to one of them and asked them where I needed to go.

He looked down at me. "What's your last name?"

"Montoya," I said, staring off into the distance behind him.

"Okay, take your bags over to the table here off to the

eastern side of the box. It has the letters on it M through O." He said, with a grin on his face.

For some reason, all of the smiling from these guys didn't put me at ease. I felt like this was their attempt at hiding what this place was like, because all of the parents being here. I was betting a lot of them would change drastically from today to tomorrow and go from being really nice people to total pricks.

I did as the cadet instructed me to and took my bags to the table that he had pointed out to me. Sitting there were two cadets, both with only two stripes on their shoulders. One was a young guy, maybe sixteen years old, and the other, an older girl about my age. She was by far the best looking girl I had seen on this campus. Hell, she made Ashley look hideous. She was a smaller girl, not much taller than 5'2" with gorgeous blue eyes that caught my attention. Her uniform was a bit tighter on her body, displaying her hourglass curves.

"What's your name?" she asked in a soft voice, looking into my eyes.

"Rocky Montoya," I responded, somewhat hesitating.

She smiled and looked down at some papers. I snagged a glance at her name-tag, reading Phillips.

"Ok, it looks like you are in Hotel Company, just over there," she said while pointing over to where Hotel was located. "Just head over to the first sergeant standing near the stairs, and he will tell you where to go next. He is the one with the round hat, and looks pissed off for no reason whatsoever."

My mouth suddenly dried up. "Thank you," I croaked, "I'll see you around."

"I'm sure of it."

Holy shit. Did she mean anything by "I'm sure of it," or

did she say that to every one of us newbie RATs. Just meeting her made me feel better about this whole damn process.

I took my bag and sauntered over towards the guy standing near the stairs with the round hat. He was a very intimating figure, two inches taller than me, around 6'5", and a very muscular guy. I wondered if he was the stud of the football team. His hair was cut so you could see his sunburn head, and he had one of the cleanest cut shaves I had ever seen. Not only was he well put together, but his uniform looked damn near close to perfect. He made me really nervous as I walked up to him. "Um, I was told this is where I'll be living this year."

"Name?" he asked, without even looking at me.

"Rocky."

"Your first name is irrelevant on this campus, what is your last name?" He gave one of the first honest responses I have felt thus far.

"Montoya."

"Ah, the Texas quarterback who thought it smart to pop a cop?"

My eyebrows shot up and my stomach nearly emptied out on his face. "How do you know that?"

"Let's just say I do my homework on all of my RATs. Take your bags and follow me." He walked with me up the first flight of stairs, me following close behind him.

"Ok, Montoya, you will be staying in H201. You are the first to show up so I might as well give you the broad overview on this all works. You will be put into a squad. Your squad will be made up of approximately five people. Four squads will make up one platoon. Two platoons will make up this company, you following me?"

"Yes, sir." I said in a quick response.

"Do not call me sir, I am not an officer. Never again call me sir."

"I'm sorry, I didn't know."

"Just don't do it again."

We arrived at H201. "This is where you will be staying." He pulled out of his pocket several keys and fiddled with them until he came across one with a tag with H201 engraved in it. He handed me the key and I opened the door to my new home.

Inside the green door was a small room with bunk beds on each side. Each bed also had a desk. Further back in the room there were two closets for uniforms, and two sinks closer to the door to wash-up. This was to be my new home and it was not something I remotely looked forward to. I just wanted out.

"Here is a DRI list." The first sergeant said handing me a piece of paper with a list on it.

"DRI list?" I asked looking at the paper.

"Dress Room Inspection list. Every day your room is expected to meet the cleaning standards on this list. Your room will be inspected on a daily basis by our Company Officer, the adult in charge of Hotel specifically. Trust me you will get used to it." He scratched his head. "Your roommate should be getting in later. You guys can get to know each other better tonight. Other than that, that is all you need to know at this point, but you will be given further instructions as the day goes on. Since you are here earlier than most you can go ahead and move onto the next stage of your matriculation. Go to the cadet store to get your standard issued uniforms. There are a bunch of signs throughout the campus to lead you there. You should be able to find it pretty easily."

"Ok, thanks," I said.

"One more thing. You're going to come out for the football team?"

"Don't know if I can." I said.

"If you want to find out, make time to speak to the coaches today. There are also signs to the locker room throughout the campus to show you where to go."

"Really? Thanks for the info."

"No problem."

As I headed outside of the box, I realized I hadn't gotten the first sergeant's name. I kind of liked the guy, even though I barely met him. He seemed honest, like a no bullshit kind of person. After dealing with all of those kiss-asses in Texas, it was nice to meet someone who appeared to be real.

The sergeant seemed different from a lot of the other cadets running around campus, with their fake smiles. The first sergeant had put in my mind that it was not going to be all smiles all the time, and a lot of these people took the military part of this school very seriously. I made a mental note not to cross people, or I could end on the wrong end of a short stick and on my way to jail. As bad as things were at Hagerman, I knew jail would be that much worse.

As I walked around campus I followed a sign pointing me to the cadet store as my first sergeant had instructed me. I noticed that more and more people were walking around the school trying to figure out where they needed to go.

Many of the incoming cadets gathered together in a group following one or two cadets in uniform. Then there were groups of parents being led by junior college cadets. I was one of the only ones walking by myself, but I didn't really mind it.

I figured this was probably going to be one of the last times for the next three weeks that I was going to be going anywhere without the permission of someone else, and I planned on enjoying it. I finally made my way to the cadet store. I walk through the two glass doors of a brick building, the first not to have a castle like architecture.

There was a long line of guys like me in normal clothes very similar to mine, indicating that they were also incoming cadets. I tried to turn around, not wanting to stand in a line that was almost out the door, when a voiced called out.

"Where the hell do you think you are going RAT?" the voice behind me shouted in my direction

"I figured I would come back when the line was shorter."

"You figured? What makes you think you have the right to figure anything anymore?" I began to feel pissed off and felt like punching the guy's lights out. The "Old Rocky" from Premium, Texas probably would have done just that. But the "New Rocky" had learned one thing from the whole cop experience. There were consequences in life for not controlling one's anger, basically jail in my case. I wanted to stay out of jail so I decided in best to play along with this dude's little image.

"You're right," I said, not recognizing my own voice. I looked him straight in the eye. "I'll get in line right now."

"Stand in line at parade rest," he told me handing me a sheet of paper and a small book. "Memorize what is written on the sheet of paper. Do not ask any questions, and do not speak. When the line moves come to attention walk until the line stops, and go back until parade rest. Do so until you reach the front of the line."

I walked up to the guy at the end of the line and imitated

the position that each person stood in, assuming that is what he meant by parade rest. My feet stood a little bit wider than natural, and I placed my left hand behind my back. I held the paper out in front of me and began to memorize its contents. I recognized that it was a list of the ranks and what core positions each rank potentially could hold.

It took me a while but I was able to get the idea of who had higher rank and who didn't, with the highest ranking cadets having more stripes unless they were officers, than they had those shiny pips on their uniform.

"Stand up straight, straight ahead, don't look at me look at your sheet of paper!" they kept on shouting. Maybe I should have just gone to jail instead of dealing with these assholes.

As I was going over the ranks again, a voice whispered in my ear, "You're sort of interesting, you know."

I recognized the voice of Phillips, the girl who had instructed me to my company.

"And why is that?" I whispered still staring straight ahead.

"You're not nervous. In fact, you look almost annoyed to be here," she said in a sweet tone.

"Why should I be nervous?"

"I was very nervous when I was standing where you are. Most people around look like they're ready to break down. But not you."

"I've dealt with worse than a couple of power hungry kids."

"I bet you have. Keep up that spirit, it will help you, and try not to get kicked out, I enjoy trying to figure you out."

"I will do my best," I said as she walked out of the Cadet Store.

Now I had something here at Hagerman to look forward

to. Next time I saw the beautiful Phillips, I needed to remember to ask her what her first name was.

After an hour of standing in line, I finally reached the front of the line where an older woman took me through the doors. I followed her into another room, sliding the sheet of paper into my back pocket. She pulled out some measuring tape and began to take some measurements of my body to see what my size was.

"Wait here," she said, as she walked out.

I stood in the room with another incoming cadet. He was a lot younger than me, maybe fifteen years old. Sweat fell from his forehead as he stood nervously waiting for a different woman to come back from the separate room. A part of me wanted to say something to calm the poor kid down, but I feared I might get in trouble. At this point in my matriculation process I realized that the weed out process had already begun. They were all trying to scare the shit out of us. Only the strong were going to survive these first three weeks. All the smiles and yes sirs and yes ma'am's and kissing ass was all a bunch of crap. What was really going down here was we were going to live in a dog-eat-dog world and I needed to be strong and suck it up. The woman that had brought me back reappeared from the room holding a red duffel bag with the name "Hagerman" written on it. The bag was full with something, but I couldn't tell what was in it. She handed it to me and said, "Go around the corner to the bathroom and try everything on to make sure it first."

I went to the bathroom and did as she said, trying on every uniform that was displayed to us last night. I emerged from the bathroom and told the woman, "It all fits."

She gave me thumbs up. "Go back in the main room with the other cadets and tell one of them you are all set." I slowly walked from the dressing area, with the duffle bag hanging over my shoulder. The young kid who was standing next to me earlier was gone.

I turned the other way and walked from the dressing room, where there were still incoming cadets standing at parade rest. As I headed to the entrance of the cadet store where other RATs had finished being issued their uniforms, a fight broke out between a uniformed cadet and a RAT. The two wrestled around for a few minutes before being broken up by other uniformed cadets. They escorted the RAT out of the store. I guess that's what Phillips meant by not getting kicked out so soon.

I walked to the entrance of the Cadet Store where there were a group of seven incoming cadets holding duffle bags over their shoulders. Once I arrived, a younger cadet, not much older than sixteen told us to follow him. For some reason, I knew he was not a prick like the others. Maybe it was a softness to his voice.

We followed him out of the cadet store into a separate building with the words "Hinkle Hall" written over it. Once we walked through the doors, the guy in uniform, asked us to form a line and to follow him downstairs into the basement of the building.

I was at the very back of the line looking around Hinkle Hall to try and get a grasp of my new home. As we moved down the stairs, I notice that up the stairs was a restaurant for cadets. It had a bright red sign that said, "PX." When we had reached the bottom step there was a long line of incoming cadets and three cadets in uniform observing us. Next to where we were standing was a game room with couches and a TV with multiple Xboxes plugged in. Beyond the games, there were bowling lanes.

I began to realize there were a lot of pain-in-the-asses bossing us all around, but they sure had amazing facilities that were beyond my comprehension.

We all waited quietly for what seemed like an eternity to reach the front of the line. I had no idea what we waited for until I entered a small room with a lot of hair on the ground. A small old woman told me to sit down in her chair. Next thing I knew she was buzzing all my hair off. She smiled at me in the mirror. "Where you from?"

"Texas."

"No kidding. Me, too. What part?"

"Premium. It's a small town."

"Yeah, I know it. I am from Dallas though. I always liked the smaller Texas towns. Probably why I ended up in Roswell."

"I don't know anything else outside of small towns."

"So why did you decide to come here to Hagerman," she said. "You look older than most incoming cadets."

"Really?"

"Oh, yeah. Most are freshman. We get few transfers."

I winked at her. "I decided it was time for a change."

"You want to go into the military huh?"

"I don't think that is for me."

She furrowed her brow. "Hmm, that don't make sense."

"I, uh, just needed to get out of Texas for a little while."

"It takes a very brave person to transfer to place like this after experiencing what a normal high school is like."

"Thank you," I said, not really knowing what else to say.

"Don't get me wrong at all, I think Hagerman is fantastic place. It turns boys into men and you will get more out of this year than you ever have in your entire life."

"I hope so," I said.

"All right, I'm finished."

"That fast?"

"It's not like I am giving you a perm and we need to be here all day," she said grinning.

I turned around and took a look in the mirror. I didn't even recognize my reflection. I looked idiotic. At first I felt angry but then I rationalized that it didn't really matter what I thought. When I walked into the hall and looked at every other RAT who had just gotten their haircut it hit me, that we all looked identical.

Once again, I kept thinking how much I regretted hitting that cop and how badly I wished my only concern in the world was school and football. But that was no longer my reality, and on this day my new life began. If I did not want it to get any worse, I was going to suck this all up and play their game.

I picked up my duffle bag and continued on out the door with the seven incoming cadets I had walked in there with. There was a different guy to lead us to our next spot. I could tell by the look of this guy he was a real dick.

"Get your shit and let's move it. Don't think we are on your schedule RATs, hurry up!" he said to the group of us.

He started yelling at us not to walk but to march. None of us had learned how to march, but this jerk did not care one bit. He tried to teach us how on the fly but it was a complete disaster. "Left, right, left, right, it's not that hard! What so hard about it?" he yelled up and down the line.

We all just stood in silence not knowing if we were supposed to answer his question.

"Since you are all acting like a bunch of retarded mutes, I will show you," he shouted. "'Left' means left foot hits the ground, 'right' means right foot hits the ground. It's not that hard. Shall we try it again?"

Again we stood in silence before he turned us and we started marching again. It was not long before he stopped us all again. "My God, you all must be slow. See this," he said holding up his fist. "It's a hand. What we do with this if we cuff it and move it opposite our foot. Let's try again."

And once again we were marching. I didn't like his tone at all. It was really starting to get under my skin.

The guy was a little bit smaller than me, but not nearly as muscular. He had pale skin and as his screams got louder, his face became redder.

His yelling became louder with every step we took but he was no longer correcting our marching but insulting every one of us individually. There were some kids who were really young, fifteen or sixteen. Two young girls in line with me kept their heads down not wanting to attract any attention. One of the girls was on the verge of tears.

All of us headed over to what looked like an armory. Incoming cadets shuffled out of the building holding rifles over the opposite shoulder of the one holding the duffle bags. We had almost reached the building when the Sergeant yelled. "Stop, you imbeciles. Don't go on the grass."

We all halted immediately and began to look around for instructions on what to do next.

"Don't move," said the Sergeant. He ran into the building. Everyone looked like they were ready to piss their pants. At this point, I just felt tired and annoyed. I had dealt with people like this Sergeant before and I was sick of his attitude, like he was a God or something. I was especially annoyed that he kept yelling at the two girls next to me on line. One of them had tears in her eyes. I leaned over to her and whispered, "Try and pull yourself together. He was keying on you 'cause he knows you're scared of him. If you can control your emotions he will find someone else to go after."

She gave me a cute smile. "I'll try. And thank you."

"What the fuck is going on out here!" the Sergeant yelled as he came out of the building. "Why are people out here talking? You have lost the right to speak without permission the moment you walked onto this campus. You all are RATs, so do you know what that means?" He stopped right in front of the girl that I had whispered to as he asked this question.

She tried to look down, but the asshole took another step toward her getting right in her face. Again he asked, "What about you, do you know what that means? It means you shut your fucking mouth!"

As he yelled at her, I wanted to say something to defend this girl in some way, because I was the reason she was getting yelled at. If I had not said anything, she would have been left alone. I understood that yelling came with the whole military thing. But there was a line at a school that wasn't training soldiers, but just educating young people, like this fifteen-year-old girl. And this Sergeant, whose name-tag read Torrez, was a grown man.

I managed to contain myself and not say anything to Sergeant Torrez. He took a few steps back. "They aren't quite ready to distribute your new weapons to you just yet, so we are going to play a little game."

I had a feeling he was going to continue on with his power trip. "Let's see how much each of you know. The questions I ask you, you better answer correctly or it will end badly for you. The questions I will ask will be from the sheet of paper given to you that you should have memorized by now." He walked up and down the line of us, each of us facing him. He stopped in front of a guy around my age and asked him what his rank was. The guy froze, looking into Sergeant Torrez's eyes.

"Get down, and knock out twenty-five push ups," he said walking away from him. The guy got onto his hands and knees in the grass and began doing push ups.

Sergeant Torrez continued strolling up and down the line and then zeroed in on the girl he had just yelled at. He looked into her eyes with a smirk that made me cringe. "What about you sweetheart, do you know what my rank is?"

The young girl looked down her eyes welled up with tears. She had no idea what the three stripes over his shoulders indicated. Sergeant Torrez's smile grew wider and before he could tell her to do pushups I shouted, "Sergeant."

I knew speaking out of turn would really piss him off. His attention turned away from the young girl and onto me. But that was my plan. I could handle this prick.

He took two steps in my direction and got right in my face. "The fuck you say?"

I didn't show fear even though I was sweating bullets.

"Your rank is Sergeant," I said with a firm and strong voice, looking him dead in the eye.

"I know what you said RAT, I'm not retarded." He looked

me up and down. "I want to know what makes you think you can speak when not spoken to, RAT?"

"I thought it was a universal question, Sergeant." I said, maintaining the firmness in my voice, never losing eye contact.

"What had I just told your little friend here? I told her not to speak until spoken to."

"Then when you ask a question from us, make it clear that it is not a universal question, instead of just standing in front of one us."

"You have an attitude you piece of shit RAT?"

"No, but I think you do."

"You better shut your fucking mouth, or I swear to God I'll shut it for you."

When he threatened me, my fist began to clench. I had never wanted to hit someone more than that moment. But I controlled myself. I knew if I hit him they would throw me out of this school so fast it would make my head spin. So instead I continued to stare at him when moments after he had threatened me, I let out a bark imitating a dog.

"What are you a dog now?" he asked folding his arms.

"No, but I'm curious if you're going stand all afternoon barking at me like a doggie, or are you going to bite?"

He scratched his head. I knew he had no idea what to do and was beside himself that someone stood to him in front of the group. I doubted anyone had ever stood up to him before.

He literally froze.

Several other RATs standing throughout the line let out the crack of a laugh. He started to step toward me when an adult at the front of the armory yelled, "Torrez, we are ready for your group."

Torrez told us all to get into the armory quickly, his face as red as a strawberry.

When I passed him, he grabbed my arm and whispered, "This ain't over. I will see you again very soon, Rat."

I shrugged him off and followed the group. One of the guys in front of me looked back and said, "You are one bad ass, dude."

We ate lunch together around noon and I realized that the lines were growing longer, due to the fact that a lot more incoming cadets were well into the process of matriculating.

Eventually, I met my senior academic advisor, who helped me select the required classes for me to graduate on time. After that, I sat in a classroom with twenty or so incoming cadets and watched a video about what Hagerman called the honor code. The video explained that if we did not abide by the honor code, which meant no cheating, lying, and stealing, we would be expelled from the school. No second chances. No tolerance policy. The remaining stations dragged on for hours and I felt like the day was never going to end.

By four o'clock, I had completed the matriculation process and was told to return to my company area. I headed back to Hotel Company and found my room and opened the door. I was exhausted from all of the constant walking around and being always told what to do. I didn't feel like unpacking but I knew I might not get another opportunity, so I removed everything from my suitcase and put my clothes in the closet space provided.

That's when I saw the suitcase sitting on top of the bed opposite mine. I had never had a roommate in my life and hoped he wasn't a jarhead like a lot of these people running around in uniform. If he was, I doubted we'd ever get along. I hoped he might be more like me. Someone not all rah-rah about being in an insane place like this, and a guy who was into sports. If he was a football player, that would be a big bonus. I assumed he was still in the process of matriculating and did not think we would meet until tonight.

Just then the door opened and a tall kid stood before me. He was a bit of a pretty boy, with bright blue eyes and blonde hair. He had a strong build. His duffle bag was strewn over his shoulder and he held his BDU's in the other hand. He looked exhausted. Worse than me, if that was possible. He walked right by me and threw all of his stuff to the ground next to the closet opposite mine. "Fuck me," he said, and then sat down on his chair. Finally, he glanced up at me. "Do you think they just want to kick the crap out of us on the first day by running us around? Or do you think it is more for their entertainment?"

"I couldn't tell you, but it's obvious they think they're gods."

He laughed "Good answer. My name is Brett." He held his hand to shake mine.

I returned a hand and shook his. "Rocky."

Brett rolled his eyes. "So what do we do now? Just sit around until they call us." I could tell we were going to get along just fine. What a relief. He was my kind of guy.

"That is what I assume, I said. You a senior?"

"I am indeed. My father is in the Air Force, and he just got stationed at the base in Albuquerque. He has a thing for military schools so I have been in them my whole life."

"So you're into all of this military stuff," I asked with a bit of hesitation.

"Fuck no, I hate it, but my pops told me I won't have to

worry about college expenses if I go where he tells me until I graduate, which I am cool with. I can deal with these kids for another year, but once I'm done I'll never put on another uniform. What about you, Rocky? You into all of this stuff?"

"Are you shitting me? This is my first time doing anything remotely like this."

"Why come here your last year in high school? Did you wake up one morning and say hey I want to be yelled at and forced out of bed at ungodly hours for kicks?"

I debated how to answer his question for a minute. "Court order actually."

"Nice," he said, smiling and shaking his head up and down. "What did you do?"

"I'd rather not say."

"Oh come on, it's not like you're the first court-ordered guy I have met at military school."

It was hard to get out. I sat there for a few seconds then finally decided I might as well get the thing over with. "I got drunk, then hit a cop after getting pulled over. If that wasn't bad enough I made a run for it."

"Like you just hauled ass out of there or what?"

"I jumped into my car and tried to out run them. Three cars ended up chasing me."

His smile grew as I spoke. His eyes opened wide. He appeared infatuated with what I was telling him. "Dude, remind me not to fuck with you."

The two of us laughed and I moved onto the chair next to him. "So if you're not a jar-head and you aren't into all of this, what's your thing?"

"I am your standard guy. I am a basketball and baseball guy, but where my talents supersede everyone else is in football." The way he said it there was a bit of arrogance in his voice, but mostly confidence. Something I liked in a person.

"Me, too," I said.

"You're a football player?"

"You bet your ass I am, and not a bad one at that."

"I hope you aren't a receiver, because I would hate to be responsible for you sitting on the bench all year," Brett said with a smirk.

"Never really had the hands to be a receiver, but I am quarterback."

"You any good?"

"You can tell me after the first day of practice, that's if they let me play."

"Why wouldn't they let you play?"

"Well, since I am here on court order and this is more of a punishment for me, I'm not so sure on how the rules work."

"Ah, dude, no worries. They will let you play. I have met a bunch of people who have been court-ordered to places for stuff worse than what you did, and they all were allowed to play sports."

I felt like a massive weight was lifted off of my shoulders. Everything thus far at Hagerman was so foreign to me. The fact that everything was so different made football that much more important because it was something familiar and something I was good at. I finally felt things might be turning around. I really liked my roommate and I'd be playing football. Life could be worse.

Moments later, the First Sergeant shouted, "All RATs fall out and to line up in the grass."

Brett and I walked out of our rooms, down from the stairs and clustered around the First Sergeant in the grass area in front of our company

Standing next to the First Sergeant was an older female cadet and also a Latino cadet. "We are still missing two RATs, but the majority of you guys are all here and ready to go," the First Sergeant said looking at all of us. "For those of you who have not met me yet, I am First Sergeant Archie. I know it has been a long day for you all. Everyone wearing a uniform has gone through the same process as you and has thought the same thoughts you are thinking now. I assure you this day is almost over but there is one more thing that some of you need to do before dinner. For high school RATs interested in fall sports now is the time to get you signed up. Staff Sergeant Schwartz here will take the ladies to meet with the woman's volleyball coach. Private Lopez will take those interested in soccer, and I will take those wanting to play football. Junior college athletes will meet with their coaches tomorrow afternoon. For those of you who are not interested in sports, go back to your rooms and change into your PTs. The red uniforms if you forgot, and make sure not to forget your RAT sox and RAT hat. We will be calling you all out for supper roll call, or SRC, in an hour and a half. Take this time to relax. Trust me you're going to need it."

Brett and I, and a young looking RAT, followed the First Sergeant out through an opening on the eastern side of the box to a building standing parallel to the eastern walls of the dorms. This building was also very long, nearly as long as one side of the dorms. It was built completely of brick and at the far end near Honor Street was a white door. There were about a dozen guys walking through the white door, all with identical buzz cuts, indicating they were RATs too. We walked in and closed the door behind us.

There were red images of a colt drawn one side of the brightly lit hallway. We made our way to the locker room, down a hallway lined with pictures of past football players, wearing the distinct red jerseys and black pants with the colt displayed on their helmet.

First Sergeant Archie poked his head into the coach's office. "I got me three RATs who want to sign up for football."

"Bring them in," he said. I was the first to enter. I walked up to a desk where an older man sat who I assumed was the head coach. He looked like he was living in his sixties as he wore a red collared shirt with the same colt logo on it. His shirt was tucked into plaid shorts that were pulled up fairly high over his waist. He had on a small hat with the colt logo stitched onto it. I stared at his bushy mustache.

He looked up at me and drawled with a distinct southern accent. "Name, boy?"

"Rocky Montoya," I said looking down at the floor.

"Son, I am not down there, look at me. I ain't like them military people, you can relax in this locker room. Call me, Coach Lou. What year are you?"

"I'm a senior, coach."

"Ever play any ball before, or is this your first time?"

"I played football all of my life back in Texas."

"A Texas boy, huh? Then you better be a football player. What position are you? You look big enough to be a linebacker and tall enough to be a receiver."

"I am a quarterback, sir. I started all three years down in Premium."

"Is that so," he said looking me up and down. "Well, we will see about that. Go into the locker room down the hall and you will find a kid with a Colts hat running around. Tell him that you need a QB number, anything less than 20. He will also fit you for your pads, helmet, and shoes if you ain't got any. You got all that?"

"Got it."

I walked down the hall leaving everyone in the coach's office. When I entered into the enormous locker room I was blown away. The perimeter of the room was made up of black lockers, with a comfortable chair at each one. The locker room floor was made up of red carpet with the Colt logo at the center. The locker room chairs all faced a screen and a film projector.

I found the guy who Coach Lou was talking about in a back room where all of the equipment was stored. It took me about ten minutes to make sure I got all of the proper equipment. The guy told me to pick any locker that didn't have equipment hanging from it.

The locker room was half full in the middle were a few open lockers. I stood next to the locker that was now mine and began to hang up my pads.

Moments later, the young cadet and Brett were both putting their equipment in the lockers next to mine. As we finished up, Coach Lou walked in and handed Bret a roll of tape and a black marker. "Write your last name on the tape and stick it over your locker," he said. We all did and then proceeded down the long hallway to meet up with our First Sergeant. As I left the room, I noticed the last locker, near the door had a piece of tape with the name Archie written on it.

Soon, we were back in the box and in our room like everyone

else. Brett and I changed into our PTs, as we were instructed to. There was nothing for us to do except put sheets on our bed and unpack as we waited in anticipation for what was to happen next. All of our electronics had been taken away in the matriculation process. We had no phones, no computers, and no watches. All we had was a closet with our normal clothes in a drawer, and several uniforms hanging. At our sink, there was only a toothbrush, toothpaste, and deodorant. There was nothing else to do but get to know each other. Brett and I chatted about ourselves.

It had been a relatively good day. I was thrilled that I'd have the opportunity to play football. I knew that impressing scouts again was a long shot, but I was grateful to get some normality back in my life. My roommate and I hit it off and it looked like we were both going to be good friends. I also took pleasure in knowing that my first sergeant was not an asshole like a lot of the others wearing round hats. I had not yet met anyone, other than Brett. I had no idea who my squad leader or platoon sergeant was. After memorizing the rank sheet when matriculating, I realized I'd be in contact with those two the most. But I wasn't too worried about that right now, mainly because of how tired I was. As the night carried on we were not allowed to leave our rooms, other than to go to the bathroom, three doors down, so we got into our bunks and tried to sleep, completely unaware of what was yet to come.

Chapter Four

The following day, I awoke to a blaring sound over the loud speaker that resonated through the barracks. All I could make out was the song, "Welcome to the jungle, we got fun and games." At the same time, the cadets were banging on each of the doors at each dorm level and repeatedly yelling, "Get your asses out of bed and fall out!"

I jumped from my bed and landed on the floor, nearly hitting my own chair, still half asleep. Brett and I raced to our closets and pulled out our RAT uniforms. I put on the black shorts, tucked my red shirt into it, and slipped on the hideous RAT socks that went clear up to my kneecaps.

"Talk about pandemonium," I said to Brett.

"This ain't too bad. Better than them coming into our rooms and dumping cold water on us, in our sleep."

"Shit, they did that to you at your last military school?"

"Nah, my buddy said they did that to him on their first morning up in Colorado, but he went there for bad behavior."

My stomach turned a bit hearing this, being that I wasn't exactly here at Hagerman for the best of behavior.

I placed the red RAT hat on and sprinted out my door with

Brett. We both ran down the stairs as everyone around kept on yelling at us to get into formation.

First Sergeant Archie shouted, "Two platoons, three squads in each platoon. Each squad should have five RATs in them, only one should have six."

Others shouted different things at the same time, making it impossible to really hear what each of them wanted from us. The officers standing in front of us on the grass were junior college students. With straight faces they watched us scramble to a spot. "This formation will be your squad until you are told differently," said the cadet with three silver circular pips on his hat. Brett explained the pips indicated that he was our Captain and Company Commander the previous night.

"This is bullshit, everyone get down and knock out pushups. Right now!" said the Sergeant First Class, in the other platoon.

All twenty-five RATs in that platoon performed push-ups while the Sergeant shouted, "Take off your fucking hats and put them in front of you! Do not stop pushing on that ground until I tell you stop!"

The platoon I was in was organized for the most part and our platoon sergeant was not as aggressive as the other one who had just dropped his entire platoon.

I glanced at my squad leader who stood three RATs over from me. He was a tall and kind of goofy looking guy with curly red hair and an array of freckles on his face.

He didn't intimidate me. As I peeked around me, one of the other old cadets glared at me. "What the fuck are you looking at?" I shot a quick glance in his direction and realized it was Sergeant Torrez.

"Mind your own RAT, Torrez and leave mine to me," my

squad leader yelled back at Torrez. The Sergeant walked up and stood in front of me, looking me straight in the eye. "Trust me, today is not the day to make a name for yourself. Keep your eyes straight ahead and do not speak unless spoken to you. Do you understand me?"

"Yeah," I replied, momentarily forgetting I was at Hagerman.

"Yes, Sergeant," he snapped back me.

"Yes, Sergeant!" I said.

Sergeant Torrez already had it out for me and I knew it best not to make any more enemies this early on. There was constant commotion throughout the box. Every other company was doing the same thing as we were and from any view, we'd look like a shifting storm of red shirts and black shorts. All of the other cadets were yelling at their RATs, some worse than others. You could see scattered groups of RATs cranking out pushups. It was pandemonium.

The song was still blaring throughout the area, and I knew I would always associate that song with my first morning in this hellhole. The smell of wet grass added to the feeling of chaos. I had no idea what time it was.

After about fifteen minutes of being shouted at, a loud trumpet sounded from a speaker. The screaming suddenly stopped and those in uniform fell into the same formation we were in. The officers took their positions in front of us with the Captain next to a private who held a white flag with the red letter "H".

For a moment, there was complete silence. Then, from the main entrance of the box, I heard someone shout orders to all companies.

The voice shouting the orders I recognized as the Regimental Commander. He stood in front of a group of older cadets who were more than likely on par to his Regimental Staff. At this point, every other cadet stood looking straight ahead, standing at the position of attention, not moving a single muscle.

"Left face," The Company Commander yelled after the Regimental Commander had concluded. Every other Company Commander followed suit ordering a left face. An orchestrated routine followed. Those on the opposite end of the box ordered a right face, forcing all companies to face the main path. The Company Commander, along with the Private holding the flag, walked to the very front of all of us. I noticed that a lieutenant, our Platoon Officer, walk past each platoon. The Platoon Sergeant hustled to the left side of each platoon, and the First Sergeant moved in between both platoons but stood about five feet away, allowing him to see the whole company and shout orders.

Once everyone was in position, the Company Commander cried "March!" The moment this happened, First Sergeant Archie shouted, "Left, left, left, right, left."

I struggled somewhat with marching at first. As we moved forward, my platoon sergeant shouted at me. "Get in step, Montoya!"

I felt my face redden then finally figured it out after First Sergeant Archie looked at me and yelled, "Left, right, Montoya."

Duh. I stepped down with my left foot and then did the same with my right. My Platoon Sergeant then focused his attention on others struggling with the cadence. I kept my head straight ahead, my hands cuffed, like I was holding a roll of quarters and made sure to listen to the cadence. "Keep in step, every time your foot hits the ground the opposite arm should be swinging forward," the Platoon Sergeant yelled.

We marched out of the back of the box on to Honor Street. Our company was the next to last company to leave the dorms, as each fell out by alphabetical order. I had no idea where we were marching to or what these guys were going to make us do. No information had been relayed to us. I whispered to Brett who stood in front of me. "Where are they taking us, dude?"

He just shrugged.

They clearly did not want us to know. The companies in front of us marched up the bridge that crossed over the main street in Roswell. It was still dark outside and only a few cars were traveling underneath the bridge.

We made our way down the bridge past the baseball stadium. Beyond the stadium was a large field with a circular dirt path surrounding it. Each company made their way to their designated area in the field and came to a stop. There was dead silence throughout the core except for the occasional "straight ahead" order given to us from behind.

Soon after, we were instructed to do all kinds of exercises, ranging from abdominals to pushups. Some of the workouts were pretty strange but they were easy for me to get through. There was a lot of yelling from the cadets who did their best to attempt to degrade each and every one of us RATs.

Thank God, they left me alone. I didn't have a problem handling exercises. All those years of football had kept me fit. After the field exercises had concluded, they lined each company on the dirt track and one by one, they sent us off on a run around the track.

First Sergeant Archie told all of us to remain in the

formation. He encouraged those of us who felt we were in the best shape to lead the squad. He looked each and every one of us in the eye. "Do not fall out or you will pay severely for it."

It soon became our turn and we all took off running. The sun began to show its face over the eastern horizon. Unfortunately, the light came with the price of the heat. The temperature rose steadily with each passing minute. It wasn't long before RATs in companies ahead of us began to fall out of formation, and stand curled over with their hands on their knees trying to catch their breath. Cadets in uniform would catch up to those struggling, "Don't stop. Catch up with your companies."

Some were able to catch up. Those not in good enough shape to maintain the pace were told to get on the ground and do pushups. I felt really bad for them. A lot of them were younger and in poor shape.

"Beal, don't stop, keep running," said Torrez.

I looked back to see who Torrez was yelling at. Beal was poor girl Torrez picked on at matriculation. She was slowing down and it did not take long for her to completely fall out of formation.

I wanted to go back and encourage her to catch up. I couldn't stand to see the twisted expression on her face.

Brett turned to me and issued a warning. "Don't even think about it. You go back to get her, those fucks will be all over you. They will probably do worse to her if you go back, man. Don't fall out."

I knew he was right but I could not help myself. Within seconds, I fell out of formation and ran back to poor Beal who was curled over, gasping.

"Come on, Beal," I said. "You can do it. Just push through and the pain will subside."

As she moved forward, I felt a hand grab my shoulder, then grip hers too. "What the hell are the two of you doing out of formation?" shouted Torrez.

"She needed to take a break, man."

"Man?"

"Just cool it. We're just about to catch up to the formation."

Torrez curled up his lip. "Can you answer a question for me, RAT? What makes you think you can talk to me like I am your buddy?"

"All right, Sergeant Torrez, whatever."

"You better learn to respect my rank and authority, RAT."

"Sure, just let go of me."

"You're not listening to me," he snarled.

"I don't think you are listening," I said. "Let go of my arm." I felt my hand curl into a fist.

His eyes blazed red. "What are you gonna do tough guy?"

I heard a voice in my head that said, "No, Rocky. Don't do it." But as if I was on autopilot, I smacked him a good one across the face as hard as I could.

He fell to the ground.

"I told you to let go." My voice was now shaky as I began to think of the consequences of this action.

First Sergeant Archie ran up to us and immediately separated me from Torrez. He glared at me. "Go form up with the company. They just finished the run. I'll deal with you later." He turned to Torrez, who had just stood up. I couldn't hear what he was saying to him as Beal and I jogged back to the rest of the company.

No one else seemed to notice what had just happened except for First Sergeant Archie, so I was pretty confident I had just dodged a bullet.

When we got back to the company, Beal whispered the words, "Thank you. I'll never forget what you just did for me."

A minute later, we marched back to the box. The Company Commander shouted, "Twenty minutes to shower and change into a new pair of PTs. Do not be late. Okay, you are dismissed."

Brett and I scurried to our room, stripped down and put on our robes. Brett headed out the door first with me behind him. Just as I was exited the door's threshold, I felt someone push me hard back into my room.

First Sergeant, Archie, closed the door behind him. I stood awkwardly as he stared at me with a red-purple face. He moved his head within inches of mine. "There are a couple things we need to get straight right now, Montoya. You are in a military environment and in a position with zero authority. You will show my cadre the respect they have earned, even if you do not like them."

"I'm sorry, First Sergeant."

"Stop saying you're sorry and start taking responsibility for what you do. You aren't a child anymore and you will not be treated like one."

I looked at the ground. "I understand."

"I don't think you do. You realize that hitting a cadre member warrants you being thrown out of this institution if I were to report this? For you, mister know-it-all, that means jail."

How did he know about that? I was shocked that he obviously knew about my history. How naïve and stupid I was to assume that Hagerman wouldn't tell my commanders about what I'd done. Why I'd been sent here. Did he know it all? The DUI, hitting the cop, the car chase? Of course he did. I wondered who else knew. My palms clammed up and my breathing intensified. For once, I was wordless. My life was at the mercy of a guy who I had just met yesterday.

CHAPTER FIVE

"How do you know I would end up back in jail?" I asked.

"I take an interest in my RATs," First Sergeant said.

I searched for right words to convince this guy to not report me. "I promise you I will never touch anyone else while here, please do not report me."

"If I were to cut you a break, you need to start getting your shit together. That means no more back talking, and you buying into the system. You start slipping and I will find a reason for them to throw you, got it?"

"Yes, First Sergeant."

"Good, now shower up, we got a busy day ahead."

I left my room grateful to not be packing my bags. I owed my First Sergeant big time and was going to do what he and his cadre said from here on out. I was finally ready to give this place my best effort.

While this morning felt like information overload, from the workout regimen to the crap food they fed us, I had no idea what today or those ahead held in store for me. We'd been led to believe that we would have the basics down by the end of the three-week period. These activities included marching with weapons, or correctly prepping our uniforms and rooms on a daily basis, and of course learning quickly what the Company Officers (an adult officer in charge of their own company) expected from us.

To be honest, a lot of the information that I received on my first day was forgotten. I thought a majority of it was stupid. Some of the fundamental information I was able to retain like the fact that there were three formations a day during the week for breakfast, lunch, and dinner. Or that we, as RATs, had to walk on the right side of every path; and when inside the box we had to run on the right-hand side of the path yelling our company sound off, which for Hotel was "I'm a pretty princess." For the most part, I thought it was useless stuff that that I just put into the back of my mind, that I was sure I would be able to recall it when the time came.

The one thing I remembered well was how the punishment system worked because if I messed that up, I had a one-way ticket to jail. My roommate explained it to me one of the first nights after a long day of training.

Brett sat on his bed eating a bag of chips. "Ok so you understand that pushups are the lightest form of punishment."

"Yeah," I said.

"The way Sergeant McCann explained it to me, it's identical to the last military school I went to," he said. "You have your range of fuck ups, right? I mean you will obviously be punished worse if you decide to take a swing at one of these dudes yelling at us, like Torrez for example, versus something like not cleaning your room properly for the morning room inspections."

I sat down in my chair. "Right."

"So if you read in that little book they gave you on matriculation, there is a list of shit you can't do without getting what they call 'stuck' if you get caught."

I pulled out my copy of the book "Wait, what page is that on?"

"It is toward the end."

"So if you do something really minor, such as not clean your room properly or if your uniform is dirty you will get stuck. Only old cadets can stick you, but new cadets can request you to be stuck."

"That's bullshit," I interrupted.

"I know, but it is what it is. And also don't forget any adult can stick you. Company Officer, teachers, or anyone else. So every day before lunch there is piece of paper telling all of us who got stuck the previous day."

"And if we get stuck, then what?"

"Than your name will be on the list with a sentence that explains what you did, and then there will be two numbers near your name. If you do something minor, it should be something like a '1-3.'"

I put my book down. "Now this is where I get confused."

"For example, if you get stuck for your uniform not properly set up, you will get a '1-3.' The first number is the physical punishment and the second number, is the number that allows for the school to keep track of your behavioral patterns and if you need to be put on a disciplinary probation."

"And the physical punishment are the tours, right?"

"Exactly. If you get one tour, you will have to march one hour. And the marching part is a real bitch from my understanding. I guess you got to get into your BDU's and march on one of the paths out in the middle of the box with your rifle on the weekend with everyone else who got stuck. So for that '1-3' you will have to march one tour. It becomes a bitch if you get stuck for bigger things, such as fraternization, with a new or old cadet. I think that one was a '10-20.'Yes,"

"So if I got caught fraternizing with an old cadet I would have to march for ten hours right?" I asked.

"Yes. of course there is the stuff you can do that will get you a '99-99', which they will probably just kick you out instead. You can only get a '99-99' if you break the honor code. That included no lying, cheating, or stealing. Do any of that shit and it's a sure ticket back to jail."

"What happens if you get put on probation," I asked.

"Your probation will last an entire academic quarter, and for that quarter you aren't allowed to leave campus, and you will be removed from any extracurricular activities, like football."

"That sucks, man," I said, again opening the book, looking for the section on disciplinary probation.

"Just keep your head down around this place. Every other military school I have been to they have been more focused on the physical punishment instead of the demerits punishment, but what can you do?"

"Football is the only thing I am looking forward to. Otherwise it's like a really nice prison where I still have to go to school. It couldn't get worse than that."

Brett chuckled. "I also forgot to tell you about the merit system. Apparently if you do stuff for adults, like teachers and what not, you can be awarded merits, which will counteract your demerit total. Hopefully, we won't get into that position.

But it's a good back up plan."

I climbed into bed. "Well, I've decided my bad ass days are over. I'm going to keep my head down and not do anything that warrants attention," I said climbing into bed.

"You better cool it with that jackoff, Torrez."

I shouted, "Fuck Torrez."

"He may be a dick, but he has stripes, which means he does have the power to screw you over. It's not worth losing football, man."

"I know." Brett was right. I needed to stop having an attitude with Torrez or I'd end up on disciplinary probation.

We were now only one week into the three-week period and I could not even begin to explain how slow that time had taken. Even though only seven days had passed, it felt like an entire month. I did take Brett's advice and avoided trouble at all costs.

In this past week I had learned what I needed to do to survive. Setting up my uniform for daily inspections and cleaning my room for the daily room inspections.

Sometimes, I struggled with marching because my mind would wander, and I would get out of step. Then my Sergeant First Class would bitch at me.

I learned where everything was throughout the campus and could easily navigate myself within its perimeters. I discovered that the restaurant on campus called the PX had decent food, which became more important to me since the food in the mess hall had become unbearable. The thing I was most excited for was to have a soda. They only let us drink water with all three meals. I was going to be allowed to go the PX and have soda in two-weeks time.

At this point, a good amount of our incoming class had quit and gone back to their homes. I noticed throughout the week, five RATs being picked up by the parents at the Company Officer's office. I did not know their names or anything about them, but I recognized their faces as they dragged their luggage behind them and headed to their cars on Honor Street. I did begin to put names to faces as the days passed and develop friendships outside of Brett.

Brett and I had become tight, but I was also starting to get to know Ashley Beal, the girl who dropped out on the first morning run here. It was a funny coincidence with her name being Ashley.

Poor kid still had yet to complete a run, which we all did every morning. She was getting better, but she never could finish with the company. No surprise she was Torrez's favorite target, and it really pissed me off when he took it too far with her, which was pretty much every day. Ashley was one of the nicest girls I had ever met and so innocent, especially since she was only a freshman in high school.

There was one more person in the core who had grabbed my attention and me hers, yet we had barely spoken a word to one another. Phillips, whose first name I learned was Karen, lived over in India Company right next to mine, so we would frequently walk past one another throughout the days. She would always smile and say hi to me, but what really caught my attention was the fact that she remembered my name after saying hi. I mean, how many names did she take down on matriculation and she remembered mine out of all of them? We would shoot a smile to one another but nothing more.

It was the night before the first day of football practice, the eighth day of hell, and for the first time I was eager to wake up the next morning. My eagerness stemmed from my desire to get back to the game that I had taken for granted. The game I realized that I loved more than anything. I stood brushing my teeth after a hellacious day of weapons training where they made us clean our weapons all afternoon.

It was close to taps when I looked out my window and noticed that two-dozen kids in civilian clothes walking through the center of the box, dragging suit cases behind them. Each headed to different Company Officer's offices.

I waved my hand at Brett. "Come check this out."

He climbed out of bed and stood next to me.

"Who are they?"

"Remember when First Sergeant told us more cadets would arrive when the sports teams started practice?"

"Yeah."

"Looks like these dudes are football guys arriving today. The day before school starts, the rest of the cadets will arrive."

I looked up at him. "The guys coming in the day before school starts can't be part of a sports team, could they?"

"No, these guys just weren't selected—or important enough—to assist matriculation. For the most part they are privates or private first classes but not higher ranks than that."

"So our Core is going to get bigger then?"

"A lot bigger," Brett said, turning away from the window.

As I climbed into bed, one thought crossed my mind. If there were more cadets that were a part of the core that meant there must be a lot more assholes like Torrez.

CHAPTER SIX

The night came and the stars shone bright in the cloudless New Mexico sky and as the hues of red, yellows and oranges appeared at sunrise, the normal Hagerman routine took place. There was a loud and obnoxious sound playing in the background with the cadets banging and kicking our doors to wake us up. I woke up just as startled as I did on the first morning. I jumped out of bed, threw on my PTs, and raced outside to fall into my squad. Soon afterward, we did our accountability checks then marched off to do our morning run and workouts.

The day moved a lot slower than the past seven days because I was just so excited to get to the afternoon. Brett was eager to throw on the pads and get onto the football field as well. Even First Sergeant Archie appeared jittery. There was an extra pep in his step like he was ready to hit someone out there. He had to put up with all of us for the last week so there was a lot that he needed to take out on someone. I hoped it wasn't going to be me, seeing that he outweighed me by at least 50 pounds.

Every hour seemed like an eternity. Then I heard the words I'd been waiting for all day. "All football players fall out of formation and follow me to the locker rooms." Brett and I, with four kids in uniform that had just arrived, fell out of formation and followed. It was so weird to feel excited about football practice. I used to resent the inevitable soreness and exhaustion of it. Now, rather than have that feeling of dread, my body flowed with energy and excitement in anticipation. I had not touched a football or pads since I blew the State Championship game last year. Besides doing something I was used to and good at, a part of me wanted to redeem myself.

I rushed into the locker room and headed straight to my locker. Guys poured through the door behind me as there were a lot more people in the locker room than I had anticipated. The room was split in half between RATs and cadets. The guys were a lot smaller than in Texas. All I cared about was impressing the coaches and grabbing the starting quarterback position. As I strapped my shoulder pads on, a young coach walked through the door and through the room to the front near the white board.

"Listen up," he said. "For all of you who do not know me, I am coach Castro, the offensive coordinator. I have a little announcement. All you old guys already know this but for you new guys there is no rank once you step through this door. You are all equal members of the Hagerman football team so I don't want to see any core stuff while in here. You earn your football stripes on the field, core stripes are irrelevant in here."

We all nodded our heads.

He continued. "Everyone clear? All right, finish getting dressed and head through the front doors across Honor Street to Stapp Field. You old guys make sure they all get out there. Be outside in ten minutes."

As soon as Coach Castro left the room, I grabbed my helmet and walked out of the room with a couple of other guys. We jogged across to Honor Street onto a large field. It was the field that I first saw when we were drove by Hagerman's campus. The field's primary use was for parade practices and actual parades, which we had not done yet, but I did not know it was also our football practice field. I went to the center of the field where all coaches were standing around with the small group that had left the locker room with me. Behind us, football players streamed out of the locker room all with their helmets on or clutched in their hands. They seemed just as excited as me.

"Give me five returning seniors at the front and the rest of you line up in front of them and knock out your stretches. Seniors you know what to do," Coach Lou cried out when the last of us had run onto the field.

Five older guys from last year's team took charge yelling for us to line it up. They stood in a row with about five yards between each of them, and instructed us on what stretches to perform. I had done these exercises a thousand times and it was nothing new to me. I stood in the middle of the stretching formation doing just as I was told.

Throughout the stretches I gazed around me attempting to get a feel for the types of players that were on the team. The guys were a lot bigger than I had previously thought as they stood around me wearing their pads. First Sergeant Archie, who was one of the five leading the stretches, looked massive with his football pads on. Brett stood a few lines to the right of me. He was a tall skinny kid, so I sure as hell hoped that he was fast.

Once we had finished our stretching, the five leaders started to clap it out. We all copied them, clapping our hands and coming together in a large huddle with one of the leaders at the center holding his hand up. We were all mimicking him, holding our own hands up.

"Today is the first practice and we need to make it a hell of a good one," he said. "We are two weeks behind every other school in our district so we need to make that up with the quality of our practice. I better see everyone giving it a 100% today and paying attention. You first years, now is your chance to hit us and get some payback, but you better be ready to get hit right back. Like coach said, there is no rank out here, we are all brothers, and today is the first step to bring home a championship to Hagerman. Our time on three, one, two three…"

And in unison we all yelled, "Our time!"

"If you are an offensive player go with Coach Castro," Coach Lou said pointing to the man who spoke to us in the locker room, earlier. "Defense with Coach Kay," he said pointing to an older coach standing behind me. "They will take care of you, now get moving."

Our cluster broke apart, dividing ourselves between Offense and Defense. Coach Castro took us to the far end of the field where he turned to us and said, "All right, if you are a lineman or a tight end you will be working on the sled with your offensive line coach, Coach Tyson," Coach Castro said looking all of us. "Coach Tyson is standing behind you, follow him."

A big chunk of the offensive group followed Coach Tyson to the sleds. Archie, who was by far the strongest of the offensive linemen group, led the group.

Coach Castro continued, "Running Backs and Receivers, you will be working out with Coach Ridley, also behind you." And just like the lineman, more players followed Coach Ridley, including Brett.

Coach Castro asked the five of us remaining. "And for the rest of you, I am assuming you all want to be quarterbacks? I only got room for three of you, so by the end of the day two of you will be working out with another group. Let's see what you guys are made of."

Coach Castro took us to a part of the field that had circular hoops. The kid who had led the break at the end of the stretches was part of the QB group. While he was almost as tall as me, he didn't have near the same muscle mass as me. The kid was an old cadet, based on his hair cut. He was a pretty boy with pale blonde hair and sky-blue eyes. You could not get any closer to the standard quarterback stereotype and the way in which he took charge, I could tell he was the starting quarterback last year. He probably was assumed to be the starter this year, making him my only real competition. All the rest of the kids in our group were younger than blonde-haired kid and me.

We had gotten to the circular hoops, which were large circular rims, with a net hanging on the back end of the hoop to catch the football. The hoops stood eight feet tall and were of standard size. "One at a time, take a football and lets check out your arms. Just do a standard three step drop and let her soar," Coach Castro said. He tossed the ball to the kid I assumed was quarterback last year. "You're first, Jimmy."

The rest of us stood off to the side as Jimmy held the ball with both his hands in a snap position, bending over, as if to pretend he was taking the snap from a center. He stood about ten yards from the hoop and yelled, "Go," as he tucked the ball with both of his hands close to his chest, preparing to throw it. Then he took three large steps back and planted his back leg into the ground, bounced forward, and let the ball fly. He drilled the ball through the hoop and into the net.

The guy had a good arm and good footwork while dropping back but he held the ball too low by his waist, where it needed to be held higher, almost near his chest. He also had a long windup, giving the defense an extra fraction of a second to get to him. The velocity on the ball was not near where it needed to be when throwing the ball at only ten yards. Ten yards is not very far, so that makes the windows smaller where you need to get the ball through. Without enough velocity, the defense can adjust to the throw and potentially intercept the pass.

Coach Castro picked up another football from the basket. "Give me someone else."

I stepped forward from the group. "I got you, Coach,"

He tossed the ball to me and I imitated Jimmy getting into a snap position. I stood there for a second and then again yelled, "Go!" I dropped back three steps knowing for sure I was faster and had better form than Jimmy. I planted my back foot, standing tall, and got the ball out of hands quickly, launching it with incredible velocity. The ball slug straight through the hoop and into the back of the net. It was the hardest I had ever thrown a ball into the back of hoop with accuracy, but I played cool and ambled to the back of the group as if that was normal for me.

Coach Castro's eyebrows raised up to his hairline. "Hell of a throw QB. Last name?"

"Montoya, Coach."

We continued with the drill for twenty minutes each of us taking a turn throwing the ball through the hoop. Jimmy and I were by far the two best quarterback candidates. There was a third kid, maybe fifteen or sixteen who played much better than the other two. As a group, Coach Castro, rotated the five us, making us throw three step drops, five step drops, throwing on the run, rolling out both to the right and then to the left. I hit every throw dead on the nose, where Jimmy missed one or two. My form, strength, and accuracy were clearly superior which I assumed made me the better of the two of us.

However, he had something I had lacked my entire football career. It was something that eluded me and held me back as a team player.

I watched Jimmy help one of the younger players who messed up with his footwork. He showed him how to move his feet then pat his back when he did it right "Now you got it, Billy," he said. Then he headed over to another of the players and helped him out with ball position. The kid fixed it on his next throw and grinned from ear-to-ear when Jimmy congratulated him.

There was a calmness about Jimmy, something that made him appear confident. In my heart I knew I lacked the confidence that emanated from him. Had I learned anything from my high school screw up? I showed nothing but a serious face. Unlike Jimmy, I didn't help anyone else out. A part of me knew that I didn't have the leadership skills but for some reason I didn't change. I just couldn't help myself. I focused everything I had to prove to Coach Castro that I was the best quarterback in terms of athletic ability, but ignored the equally important role of quarterback leadership.

After a while Coach Lou blew his whistle. "Team workout," he yelled. Coach Castro followed Coach Lou and shouted to the offensive coaches and players to come together. I knew that this was the time to show the coaches and my teammates what I had to offer. In the past, at this point in team practice we all lined up in a formation and ran some plays against a scout team, so I assumed the same was going to happen now.

Coach Castro had each of his offensive coaches pick out who they liked initially to run with the first team offense. The guys selected were mostly retuning players from what I was later told.

Jimmy stepped up immediately with the first team's offense even before the coach picked him. For someone who had been the starting quarterback his whole life, I found this annoying. Calm down, I told myself. This was the first practice and this first offensive team practice meant little to nothing. I had close to a month before our first game to prove to Coach Castro and Coach Lou that I was the best quarterback on this team.

After the first team had been selected, the coaches began naming off people followed by a two, indicating that they would be on the second team, and then further by naming more players, following them up with a three, telling them they would start on the third team. I found myself on the second team.

Coach Castro glared at us second team players as we bunched together off to the side. "Ok," he said, "The first team players have all been here, and I am going to call out a play to them. Most of you second and third teamers are first years so I do not expect you to know the plays. Pay attention to your position though, and when your team is called you will be doing the same thing. Eventually you will all have the plays memorized."

The first team knew exactly what they were doing when they huddled for the first time. They all surrounded Jimmy, who was on one knee, one step into the huddle, calling out the play that Coach Castro had just whispered into his ear.

Moments later, the huddle broke and the players lined up in a power I formation, with two wide receivers far out, a tight end lined up to the left, and a running back and full back lined up directly behind Jimmy, who was under center.

Archie was part of the first team and lined up as the center.

"Ready, set, go!" Jimmy yelled out. Once he said go, the ball was snapped into his hands and he turned around letting the fullback penetrate through the line and pretend to block someone as the line was doing, then handed the ball off to his running back. It was a simple half back dive, nothing fancy.

I called out "Huddle up!"

Once the play was over, the second team formed around me. Coach Castro whispered in my ear, "Strong right, Power I, 32 dive, on go."

I then imitated Jimmy, taking one step into the huddle made up of nearly all RATs, including Brett, and took a knee. I repeated the play what Coach Castro had just told me and then broke the huddle. I stepped up under center and barked, "Go!" I snapped the ball and handed it off to my running back who plowed through the line. A lot of the guys flew full speed, trying to prove to the coaches that they had the potential to earn a spot on the first team. I, on the other hand, just doodled through the play, knowing that I didn't have to earn the sport, because I knew I already deserved it.

The teams kept rotating with one another. The second and third teams imitated what the first team had previously done. Nearly all of the plays were simple running plays that did not interest me. I realized that I was slipping back into my old habits. For the most part, I had been humbled through my experience here at Hagerman, but on the football field I knew that I wasn't some RAT, and that here I was "the man." The entitlement had been so engrained into my mind that I simply could not help myself. I assumed if I was patient I would be on the first team. No one played better than me!

We kept on doing these plays against a pretend defense over and over again and soon I became bored. While I memorized the lingo for these plays, I wanted to be playing against an actual defense throwing the ball more often, instead of just handing it off. The defense was doing the same thing on the opposite end of the field, just running plays against an invisible offense.

Coach Lou ran back and forth between the offense and defense. My excitement for football practices dissipated as I recalled the reason to why I never looked forward to them.

As the sun descended in the cloudless sky forming reds, pinks, and orange colors across the horizon, we continued running plays. Then a whistle from Coach Lou blew, calling us all into the center of the field. We all raced to where Coach Lou stood and surrounded him, taking a knee, so those behind us could see him.

The other coaches stood outside the circle as Coach Lou addressed us. "Ok, that will be it for today. Inside is a copy of the team's playbook for each of you. Because we had you all run through a big chunk of the playbook, it should be easy review for you all looking them over tonight. We will do the same tomorrow, and the same for the next week until all of the plays have been memorized. By that time we should have a good idea of what our depth chart is going to look like. When we know that, then we still start running some offense vs. defense. The two weeks after that leading up to our first game we should be getting last year's tape of our opponent."

The players were silent as he looked around at us and continued. "I realize that these next few weeks will not be the most interesting in the world, but we need to do this in order to get you boys ready. The weight room in the gym is next door to the locker room for those of you who have not already seen it. The door will be open all day starting the day that school begins. That is when you first years will have a lot more freedom to do what you want, so if you do not have any studying to do or have a free class period you will have the option to lift some weights. Also, each day after practice, we will leave you time to get dressed and get to your companies before supper formation. There is no excuse for you not to be there, and when sticking starts happening I will be very pissed if you get stuck for being late or missing it. Trust me, tours will be the last thing you will need to worry about. Okay, break down and hit the showers, men."

We all stood from our knee, clapping our hands to motivate one another. We came together in a team huddle with Jimmy at the middle of it. He held his hand up and all of us intimated him reaching for the center, or putting our hands on the person's shoulder pads in front of us.

"Hell of a first day men," said Jimmy. "We will need this kind of effort every day from each of you if we want to reach our potential. Now do as coach said and everyone move your asses in the shower and get to formation. Let's bring the same attitude tomorrow afternoon. Our time on three; one, two, three…"

In unison we all shouted, "Our Time!" and then ran off the field towards the locker room.

A part of me knew, as good as I was, I had royally fucked up my first impression.

CHAPTER SEVEN

Classes started the next day along with the conclusion of our brutal twenty-one day orientation. All of us RATs, were now all in uniform, and cadets who were not involved in sports or the twenty-one day period, had begun to trickle onto campus and prepare for the upcoming academic year. A lot of the cadre, who had been with us for the past three weeks, stopped paying attention to us because our training was essentially over.

Other than formation, we were allowed to do what we wanted except leave campus. I felt lucky just to able to go to the cadet store and purchase my textbooks. If you had told me that I'd be excited about buying schoolbooks six months ago, I would have laughed in your face. Back then, excitement was getting drunk, smoking some weed, and getting laid.

After lunch formation had concluded, I decided to try and miss the long lines at the cadet store by skipping lunch. When the formation broke apart, I snuck off downstairs into the store. The older women whom I had seen on matriculation were the only ones present. The woman who had given me the uniform said, "Hi Rocky. Nice to see you again."

"Ah, hi," I said. It surprised me that she'd remember my name and it made me feel good. Again, I thought about how a few months ago I wouldn't' give two shits if some old woman recalled meeting me before.

I walked towards the academic area of the cadet store with my schedule in hand and began to select the books I needed. When I looked up, I noticed Karen standing directly in front of me. My heart skipped a beat when I saw her, but I didn't know why. I wasn't sure if I was nervous about her being an old cadet and that I was going to be in trouble for ditching out on lunch, or the fact that she was there.

"Looks like I am not the only who didn't feel like waiting in line," she said with a smile.

"Looks that way," I said. I felt like an idiot not really knowing what else to say.

She let out a giggle and went back to looking at books.

I cleared my throat. "Ah, what classes do you have this semester?"

"Oh you know, physics, calculus, government, the usual."

"Damn, that seems like an intense schedule."

"Well, hopefully it will be good enough to impress the admissions at colleges for next year."

I continued following her like a dumb little puppy trying to maintain some sort of conversation, Unfortunately I did not really know what else to say without coming off as a creepy guy. This was definitely strange for me, because I was so used to girls in Texas following me around, but here, everything was the opposite.

I was thinking of something else to say when she turned around. "Are you hungry?"

"I was hoping to sneak into the mess hall after this and grab something quick to eat."

"Why?"

"Well, we aren't allowed in the PX until tomorrow, and it's not like I can go anywhere."

"What's stopping you? There isn't an electric fence surrounding the campus," she said with that troublemaking kind of smirk that enticed me.

"It's not like I can just sneak off post."

"Why not?"

"Because if I got caught—"

"Then don't get caught." She paused for a few seconds then continued. "Look, you're probably sick of this crap food that they feed us every day. And someone who has been eating it for three weeks straight must be going crazy. I know this cafe near the end of town that I have been craving to go to all day. I'd like some company."

I thought about the idea for a second. If I got caught, I couldn't even imagine the trouble I would be in. But then again, this girl was the hottest girl I had met in what seemed like an eternity, and she had this attitude that I had never seen in any girl. There was something about her. I probably would never have another chance like this again if I turned her down. "Okay, why not."

As we walked out of the cadet store into an empty campus, I turned to her. "You know if we get caught walking together we will be in deep shit, because of that whole frat thing."

"You worry too much. Everyone's in the mess hall, right? We aren't going to get caught."

"And how do we get there? Just walk five miles?"

She let out a giggle. "That sounds like a terrible idea. No, I have a car."

"You have a car on campus?"

"Yeah, it's a senior cadet privilege."

I was already impressed with this girl. Not only was she gorgeous but she also had a car! A car equals freedom in my book. People that liked to break the rules and never really get caught doing so always impressed me, and I had never met a girl with that type of personality. At the same time, based on the classes she was going to be taking this semester, she was clearly no dummy.

We wandered down campus together as a light New Mexico breeze kicked up some dust. Karen was right. Not a person in sight. We made our way across Honor Street and onto Stapp parade field. Across the field was a parking lot that had cars lined up and down it. Her car was the first car at the end of the lot.

Her car, a brand new silver Lexus, sparkled in the sun at the end of the lot. She shrugged when I whistled at it then clicked the doors open. "Wanna drive?"

Nothing I would have liked better but I figured it best I didn't and slid into the passenger seat. Karen clicked on the ignition, put the car in gear and peeled out of the parking spot.

Before I knew it, we were cruising down Main Street, the same street I drove down with my aunt when I had first entered Roswell. Somehow that seemed like a lifetime ago but it was only twenty-one days. It was the first time I had been off campus in three weeks. Driving through the city of Roswell felt really cool even though I must have looked like a little kid with his mouth open.

Karen clearly found me entertaining. She randomly laughed when she noticed me smiling when I saw something as ridiculously common as a McDonalds.

She pulled into a parking lot at the TJC Café about three blocks off of Main Street, so that we would not be seen by any Company Officers who were off duty. We went inside the café and sat down in one of the chairs near a window. A tall dude ambled over with a pad in his hands. "Ready to order? He pointed up at a chalkboard in front of us. "Chicken-fried steak with mashed potatoes is the special."

We both ordered the chicken-fried steak. Being off post was awesome in itself. But sitting there with this beautiful girl who intrigued me more than I ever imagined made me feel like I'd just stepped into this dream world. We sat in the red leather booth and stared at one another, before I decided to stop acting like a guy who had never seen a girl in his life. I cleared my throat. "Tell me about yourself."

She glanced up at the ceiling for a few seconds. "What would you like to know?"

"Whatever you want to tell me. Where are you from?"

"I'm from Albuquerque. What about you?"

I told her about the town I'd grown up in Texas.

"Well, then being in a small town like Roswell shouldn't be so different from home."

"That would be true if I felt like I lived in Roswell. Being in the city right now feels like I am in another town on vacation from my new home."

"And where is your new home?"

"Well, Hagerman, of course."

She let out a laugh. "That's a little sad."

I felt hot rears under my eyelids but held back with every ounce of strength I could muster. "I guess so. It's just that I feel, well, like I'm being trapped there for an eternity."

She brushed my hand on the table. "Why would someone like you come all the way out here to enroll in a military institute?"

I looked down. Should I tell her the truth? What if it scared her off? I would never get an opportunity like this again. Yet for some reason, I decided fuck it, maybe this chick will like it. "Court order," I finally said.

She leaned into the table and her blue eyes sparkled. "What did you do?"

"Well," I started and then took a deep breath. "One night, while in a drunken state, I decided that it would be a good idea to punch a cop and get into a car chase with him and some of his buddies."

"Bullshit."

"I really couldn't make up a story like that now could I? If I was going to lie I would come up with something more believable, no?"

Karen smacked my arm and smiled.

I told her the rest of the story about losing the State Championship and how I came to hit the cop.

"You really hit a policeman?"

"Well, it sounds bad when you say it like that," I said with both of us laughing. "And you? Why would you come to a place like this?"

"My folks are divorced, and I haven't seen my dad in several years. My mom is a tad crazy so she thought it would be a wise idea to put both my brother and me in a military institution to receive our education. She liked Hagerman the best of the ones she toured, so she sent us here two years ago."

"Is your brother still at Hagerman?"

"No, he was kicked out after his first year. So it's just me."

"You like it here?" I asked.

"I mean, it sucks, but what can you do? I'm already used to this kind of lifestyle. I sneak off once in a while to get away from it all to cope with the stress. That, and cheerleading. I've seen you out there on the field you know."

"Is that so?"

"Yeah, still trying to be a quarterback for them I see."

"It's just a matter of time before I grab the position away from Jimmy," I told her as a waiter placed two plates of food in front of us.

Karen looked me directly in the eye. "I wish you the best of luck. You've got a great arm by the way."

I looked into her gorgeous eyes. "So what are you looking to do after?"

"After Hagerman?"

"Yeah."

"I plan to go and do the whole college thing. I want to get into nursing. At least I think I do."

"That sounds awesome," I said.

"What about you, Rocky?"

I hesitated, looking down at the table. "I don't really know. I haven't thought about it."

"You haven't thought about college?" Karen asked.

"No, I mean no one from my hometown goes to college. They just stick around and get a job at a local restaurant or fixing cars."

She looked back at me tuned in to every word I said. "It's a good thing than that you're here. Hagerman has some pretty good advisors who can help you with college stuff."

"I don't know if I'm what you call college material."

"You can't think like that. If that's what you think than your mind has already given up, and if that's the case you have no shot even before you have tried."

No one had ever spoken to me in such a way. Karen acted like she genuinely cared about what is going to happen to me. I was shocked, and slightly skeptical. Who was this girl? "Are you for real?"

She grinned. Her teeth were white and perfect. "Of course. You need to go see an adviser ASAP to make sure you're taking all the right classes." She scribbled some dude's name on a napkin and handed it to me. "Request to see Mr. Sutherland. He's the best counselor at Hagerman."

After we finished lunch, we drove back to the campus parking lot. As we walked down toward campus I noticed two high-ranking cadet officers hanging out together on the edge of Stapp Field, in the direction we were headed. My heart skipped a beat and my hands became moist with sweat. All I could think about was how screwed we were.

Chapter Eight

Looking back on our date, all I kept thinking about was Karen's perfect smile and those beautiful eyes. I hadn't seen her in several days since we went to lunch. I finally got my cell phone back but hadn't thought to get her number. Duh! I couldn't even text her.

When she'd noticed the officers she whispered, "Walk like nothing's going on. I can handle these guys."

She glared at me when I started to object. "You'll make it worse, Rocky."

I took her advice and moseyed along like I'd just been taking a stroll around campus. I remember looking back when I was three-quarters through Stapp field to see what was going on. Karen stood smiling and chatting amiably with the two officers. I figured she must have known them. That was the only way she'd succeeded in getting us out of the mess that could have caused us both to get in deep shit. I was one lucky son-of-a-bitch Karen knew both of the officers.

As we started our second week of school, I felt I'd become a zombie. Since the twenty-one day period had ended, my schedule had drastically changed. We no longer woke up early to do morning physical training but had to get up at six to form up and march to the mess hall for breakfast.

"Lets go RATs! Get your fucking asses out of bed! Move with a Goddamn purpose!" Sergeant Torrez would shout.

"Torrez, chill out," one of the privates said to him one morning.

Torrez turned to the guy who had dared to challenge him. "Shut your mouth, Private."

"Yelling at them like it's the first day isn't going to get you promoted so you might as well not give the rest of us headaches," the private said.

Torrez held his head up high. "And that's why you're a private."

"Dude, its six in the morning," the private continued, "chill the fuck out."

Hearing this I couldn't help but to look over and see what would happen. Most everyone began looking in their direction to see what was going to happen. A few of the other ranked cadets headed over to separate the two of them.

"I should report you to one of the company officers for this," Torrez said.

The private's face was red. "Yeah that's it, Torrez, run and tell on me. You're such a big man."

A lot of us RATs snickered under our breaths. We had been waiting for anyone to finally get in Torrez's face.

First Sergeant Archie walked in between the two of them. "All right guys, lets cool it. Everyone's tired and pissed off."

"I'm sorry, First Sergeant, but someone needs to tell Torrez to quit with this power trip. It's too early in the morning for this guy to be running around screaming at everyone. It's too early in the morning, and too early in the year to deal with his shit. These RATs aren't dogs, and in case Torrez hasn't realized this isn't the real army!"

"I'll handle it, just go form up with everyone else," First Sergeant calmly said to the worked-up private.

The private walked away clearly upset. Torrez turned to First Sergeant Archie. "What are you going to do about this insubordination?"

"Torrez, shut the fuck up," said Archie completely blowing him off.

After eating the crappy food they served for breakfast, we sauntered back to our rooms and prepared them for dress room inspection. Then it was off to class all day until three in the afternoon, followed by football practice for two more hours.

One day, as I headed down the halls in between classes, I saw Karen walking in the opposite direction. I had not seen her in days and I could barely breath. I desperately wanted a chance to hang out with her again. Did she care about me? Or had it just been a lunch date? We both had to worry about the whole frat thing. One frat stick, and I would be six demerits away from getting put on disciplinary probation. Still I was willing to take that risk to be with her even if it put me close to losing football all together.

As she walked and talked with one of her cute friends, she smiled as brightly as ever. But she just brushed by me, not even acknowledging my existence. I could even feel her uniform graze mine, but nothing, not even one word.

After she had left the hall, I slung my backpack over my shoulder and carried on to my English class. I sat in the back row wondering why she had just passed by me without even saying hello. I knew she had to worry about the frat rule like me but the classroom buildings were a lot like the football locker room and for the most part rank went out the door and we were all the same students in this building.

The bell rang and class had begun when I put my left hand into my pocket and discovered something that had not been there before. I felt it through my fingers and realized that it was a piece of paper that had been torn from a notebook. I carefully pulled it out of my pocket, looking around to make sure no one else was watching me. I was thrilled to realize it was a note from Karen. She must have slipped it into my pocket when she passed by me. My heart nearly burst.

"Sneak away after supper formation. Meet me in the parking lot. Don't get caught." At the bottom of the note was a smiley face.

The note made my day and I couldn't wait for it to end so I could go meet her. I kept checking the clock to see how much time had passed. Each class took forever to get through and football practice was by far the worst. As much as I loved football, I was more excited to meet Karen. In fact as I daydreamed about the possibilities of our date, I forgot all about the competition with Jimmy.

When we finally all came together and Jimmy broke the team huddle. I ran off the field like a little kid excited for Christmas. The whole time I was thinking that I never have been this pumped to hang out with a girl. It was a giddy feeling, something that I had never known before.

After showering and formation I managed to sneak away and make my way to the parking lot. When I got there, Karen was already standing there leaning up against her car. "What do you say we ditch out on studying tonight?" she asked.

"I say that sounds like a fantastic idea."

We got into the car and were quickly off campus on Main Street again. I had no idea where we were going but it didn't really matter. She was next to me and that's all I cared about. Karen had an ability to make me feel nervous. She also could calm me down and make me forget about all of my problems. I had a feeling I did the same thing for her.

We drove in the opposite direction of the café that we went to a week ago, heading south down Main Street. It was dark outside, but the lights of the small buildings that lay ahead of us penetrated through the night. Roswell's downtown was almost picturesque to look at. We drove through the area and came up on 2nd Street, where Karen made a right turn. We didn't say anything to each other but listened to the radio. Once in a while we would look at each other and smile. I was confident that she felt as excited as me.

Eventually, we arrived at a residential area. She then drove us off road on a dirt path and I noticed that there was nothing around us for miles.

Essentially, we were in a type of no man's land, which I found very peaceful, especially when we got out of the car. The air felt calm and cool on my face. Grasshoppers chirped around us. Karen walked to the hood of the car and jumped up on it, indicating me to follow her lead.

She smiled. "You like my smooth note idea?"

I climbed onto the hood of the car and lay back with her next to me. "I did. To be honest, when you passed by me and didn't say a word to me, I was worried. I thought you didn't want to hang out anymore."

She touched my arm with her hand. "No, of course I do. I just don't want to give anyone the impression we are hanging out. Because when people start to get that impression they begin to talk, and when they begin to talk word gets to people with sticks up their asses and then they stick us for frat. I don't know about you, but I don't like tour squad all that much."

"I have never been on it."

"Trust me," she said, "You'd hate it. "

"How did you know that you would run into me in the halls?"

"What do you mean?"

"You had the note on you didn't you. How did you know you would see me? I mean did you write it in the class before or something?"

She looked away from me and blushed a little. "This is embarrassing, but I have had the note for a while now."

"Really?"

"I hoped to run into you somewhere on campus. And because we are in different companies, I thought the classroom would be the best chance to see you. So I have had it written in my pocket since school started and today was the first time I had an opportunity to slip it in your pocket."

I now felt confident that Karen had the same feelings for me as I had for her. However, I remained cool about what she had just said and tried to make her feel a little less embarrassed. "Well, I have been wanting to hang out with you since we had lunch at TJC."

"You have?"

"Are you kidding? I had so much fun that day. It's just I have been so busy with stuff I couldn't really try and get a hold of you to ask you if you wanted to hang out. And I didn't even have your phone number."

"Let's fix that," she said sitting up.

"Fix what?"

"You having no way of getting in touch with me. You have your cell phone back I assume?"

"Yeah, yeah I got it back." I pulled it out of my pocket to show her.

She took it quickly from my hands and punched her number into my phonebook. "Maybe next time you can ask me out instead of me asking you," she said leaning back again smiling. "So you have been busy huh?"

"Oh, yeah."

"Like with school?"

"No, no school isn't that bad. It's actually pretty easy so far. I am just worried about football."

"Why?"

"You know how you said you saw Jimmy running the first team. He is still running the first team."

"I thought you said you would be running the first team by the time the season started."

"I thought I would. But it doesn't really look good for me. The season starts at the end of the week. With each passing day, I feel like he is going to get the call to start for us."

"How good is he compared to you?"

"He's good but he isn't close to my skill level, you know. I don't mean to sound conceited but I was being looked at this time last year by major collegiate programs. I guarantee no one is looking at him. It is just so frustrating because I want to start so damn bad, but he is their favorite."

"You should talk to the coaches."

"I don't know," I said.

"I am serious. Go in there and talk to whichever coach makes the decision who starts, and ask him what the deal is," she said nudging my arm. "You really are a very good quarterback. I have seen you at cheerleading practice."

"You're right, I will talk to Coach Lou tomorrow," I said feeling less stressed. I looked up at the stars. "So you watch me at practice."

She blushed. "I totally walked into that one didn't I?"

I chuckled "You really did."

The whole night I wanted to hold her hand or kiss her but I moved very slowly. It was more important I didn't blow it with her than anything in the world. I wanted her to trust me and feel comfortable. I'd never felt like this about anyone. Not Ashley or any of the girls I'd dated before her. The night felt like a mini-vacation from the realities of Hagerman. I knew something very special was happening with me and Karen and I cherished every moment we had together. But like every vacation, it had to come to an end and before I knew it were sneaking back onto campus. I made it to my room minutes before taps filled the air of Hagerman.

CHAPTER NINE

The next day after practice I quickly got dressed and hung around outside Coach Lou's office until he was alone. This was my best opportunity to talk to him about the starting quarterback position. I entered the office where Coach Lou sat behind a desk looking at stats on his computer. "You got a minute?"

"Only one. You need to get over to your formation," he said, but not looking up at me.

"I have a question about the starting roster for tomorrow night's game."

"What about it?"

"Is there going to be a final depth chart set up or something like that, to find out where we are?"

"We don't do it like that around here. You're on the second team offense during practice, isn't that right?"

"Yes, Coach."

"Well, there you go, son. You are the back up quarterback to Jimmy."

When he said that my heart sank. I'm not sure what I'd expected, but it hit me hard to find out the reality. It felt like someone had just punched me straight in the gut. A part of me felt devastated, but the other part filled with anger. His decision was total bullshit. I could run this offense more efficiently than Jimmy, and I was the better quarterback. I looked down at the ground for a second wondering what to say next.

Coach Lou finally glanced up at me. "Is there something else I can help you with, Montoya?"

I hesitated for a moment trying to figure out how to word what I was feeling about his decision. "I, ah, just don't understand that decision, to have Jimmy start over me."

"And what part of that decision do you not understand," he said in a tone that came off like he was insulted.

"Well, even though I have been running the second team offense against our second team defense, I know I'm the better quarterback. In our individual position drills I have the better arm, the better footwork, and the better body position. I can run this offense better than he can. I am the better player."

"Do you really think that is the truth?"

"I do."

"I am going to tell you where you are wrong. Overall, you have the unique skills that make you a better player, but I am not looking for the better player in my system. I am looking for the right player. Where Jimmy dominates you is in leadership. My quarterback needs to be prepared to lead this team when times are hard and especially when everything is not going as planned. So far you have not shown me any characteristics that you are up for the challenge to put the team before yourself and lead these men to victory."

"I can do that, Coach."

"That's not true, son. When the younger kids mess up, I

don't see you trying to help them out. If someone screws up in the play, all I've seen you do is roll your eyes. A good leader would make sure that one of his players doesn't make the same mistake again. Jimmy makes sure that his first team is totally prepared and ready to go each and every play. He goes the extra mile and puts in twice the effort. Where for you, your natural skills and talent make it all come easy for you. Well, in this game there will be times when all hell breaks loose and it won't be easy and you will have to dig in and find a way to win. Even though Jimmy doesn't have your skills he always finds a way to win. He did it for me last year and he will do it again for me this year. You will have to be a good teammate and support my decision and also support your starting quarterback, do you understand me?"

I had nothing else to say after that little lecture. The man had clearly made up his mind and he wasn't about to change it, no matter how much I complained to him. All that was left for me to say was, "Yes, Coach."

"Good," he said. "Now get to formation."

As I ran back to the box, I couldn't get over what coach had just told me. I knew what Coach Lou had just told me was true, but I was devastated by his decision. All I could think about was how unfair he had been. The rest of the night I couldn't concentrate. I sat at my desk staring out the window while my homework remained untouched on my desk.

Brett watched me sulk at my desk for hours while he was busy doing his homework. "Man, that's really tough," he said when I told him what had happened with Coach.

"It sucks because I know I could take this team further than Jimmy," I said.

"Well, if you keep working hard enough I'm sure you'll get your shot."

I shook my head. "Nah, Coach has made up his mind. He doesn't trust me. He thinks I will crack under the pressure."

"How do you even know you will crack?"

"It wouldn't be the first time. Listen, I don't really feel like talking about this."

I lay in bed staring at the ceiling thinking of what to do next. That night was the hardest night I endured at Hagerman. All of the other nights I was either so exhausted from the day's activities or excited for something happening the next day. But on this night none of that was happening for me. All I thought about was how much crap I'd endured the last two months. I'd been yelled at like a dog, and forced to ask permission to do everything from using the bathroom to requesting to eat. Yes, I'd gone along with their little game for fear of getting kicked out and going to jail. That night, I didn't care anymore. I no longer had football as a motivator to get through the day. There was Karen. But, we risked everything to spend time together. Sooner or later, we'd probably get caught. I didn't give a shit what would happen to me, but was real concerned what the consequences would be for her.

So what did I have keeping me here? After several hours, I came to the conclusion that I had nothing at Hagerman. It would be better for me to just to leave. If I headed out now, I'd have an eight-hour head start on them before they realized I was gone. I could catch a Greyhound bus that would take me the furthest away from here for the cheapest price. I'd start over. I'd disappear from all of my problems.

I climbed down from my bunk careful not to wake Brett.

The clock said it was one in the morning. I tiptoed to the back of the room and stuffed some things into my backpack. I couldn't take it all if I was going to sneak off campus in the middle of the night. There were night TACs all over the campus comprised of adult officers whose sole responsibility was to make sure the cadets were safe throughout the night. If I got caught by one of them, it would ruin my plan.

I needed to make my way to Stapp without being seen. If I could get to Stapp, I would become invisible, because there were no lights out there, as opposed to the rest of the campus. Once at Stapp, I would make my way to a Greyhound bus terminal.

When everything I needed was stuffed into my backpack, I slung it over my shoulder. I popped my head out the door to see if I could see any night TACs walking throughout the box. One sat in his office on the opposite end of the box, but he posed no threat to me. There were three more throughout the campus but I could see none. I decided now was my best chance, so I stepped outside my room and silently raced down the stairs. Once on the first level of Hotel, I ran for the side exit of the box. There was still not a TAC in sight and far off in the distance I saw Stapp so I made a run for the darkness. To my surprise, I didn't see one night TAC on my route to Stapp field. I thought I was home free.

At this point it did not take long to get off campus and over to the Greyhound station. I walked inside and purchased a one-way ticket to Albuquerque, which was three hours northwest of Roswell. I figured that once I was there I would be able to come up with the next step in my plan.

I knew I didn't have much of a plan and started wondering

if I'd made the right decision to run away. I had put so much into this place, a place that I thought I hated, a place that was just too hard to get through. A part of me thought about how far I had come and how much I had learned about myself in such a short period of time attending this school. Hagerman was designed to be challenging and difficult and I felt a sense of accomplishment by getting through the twenty-one day period when so many could not. I knew the type of person that I'd been in Texas, but I wanted to think that I was beginning to change and even grow up. All of these things raced through my mind at the same time.

"Someone sitting here?" an older man asked me as he sat down before I even got the chance to respond.

"All yours, buddy," I said, not really wanting to be bothered by this guy. He was a big dude, dressed in a torn wool jacket full of stains, and a pair of Wranglers that hugged his hips. He smelled like he hadn't taken a shower in a long while. In his right hand he held a brown bag wrapped around a bottle. After every swig he took, the smell of liquor on his breath got stronger.

"Where are you off to bucko?" he asked slurring his words.

I inched away from him on the bench. "Albuquerque."

"Never really liked Albuquerque that much," he said. He paused for a few minutes. I thought he was done talking but the he looked up at me again with moist eyes. "How long did you last?"

"What?"

"How long did you last at the Institute?"

"Long enough. How did you know?"

He chuckled. "Your hair was a dead give away." He took

another drink from his bottle. I began to get uncomfortable and inched as far away from him as I could.

"I went to Hagerman once upon a time ago," he said.

"Did you now?" I didn't believe him.

"Some thirty years ago. Like you, I'm a military quitter. I left after about six months into the program and have no regrets. That was the shittiest place one earth, a bunch of wannabe military kids, all with sticks so far up their ass they could barely walk."

The old drunk kept rambling on, insulting the school every chance he got. A weird thing was happening to me. While I should have been agreeing with the drunk, it was just the opposite. I began to take offense to what he was saying. Suddenly, it was clear to me I'd made the wrong decision by leaving Hagerman. I didn't want to end up a bitter loser like him. I was leaving a place that offered me the opportunity to become a better man. I began to understand that you don't improve without going through certain hardships. It's the quitters who are the losers and who are just too afraid of the "hard."

In that moment, I learned something about myself, a truth that I had never admitted. Every time something got tough in life I'd always come up with an excuse to quit or found someone else to blame.

A fire now burned in the pit of my stomach creating an incredible amount of motivation to finish what I had started at Hagerman. A desire to change for the better, and become the man I wanted to be. Deep down, no matter how hard Hagerman was, I had what it took to beat it.

After this incredible rush of motivation, I stood up as the

drunk continued to rant on. He shut up when he noticed me stand up.

"Where ya going?"

"Thank you, sir," I said.

He furrowed his forehead. "Thanks for what?"

"Thanks for allowing me to see what would happen to me if I were to run."

I threw my bag over my shoulder and rushed away from both him and the bus station. Over and over I told myself that I could do this. I would beat this place. As I returned to campus, I was so deep in thought that I forgot to check if the coast was clear. Next thing I heard was a deep voice shouting, "Hey, you over there, stop!"

I stopped in the middle of lit up sidewalk, sticking out like sore thumb, in the light. How stupid could I have been? Two night TACs raced up to me. My heart pounded harder with every step they took closer to me. Two options presented themselves. One, I could stand there and wait for these night TACs to take me to their office, where my ultimate punishment would be to put me on disciplinary probation after getting stuck for AWOL. Or two, I make a run for it and make these two guys earn their paycheck with the hope I didn't get caught.

"Fuck it," I said out loud.

CHAPTER TEN

I slung my bag over my shoulder and took off into a dead sprint down the sidewalk. The two TACs, started chasing me. I didn't know where I was running to, all I knew was I needed to get out of sight quick.

As I ran, it occurred to me I wasn't dressed as a cadet. These TACs probably thought that I was a civilian sneaking onto Hagerman's campus, which meant that they would either call campus police or Roswell police. Bad news for me either way. I needed to get into my dorm quickly before I got caught.

I bolted at lightning speed down a path outside of the box and leaped behind some bushes. The two night TACs ran right by me, struggling to breathe. I managed to make out the words of one of the TACs on the radio. "Have campus police hit the lights throughout the campus. There are a lot of dark spots out here. Get the lights on and we will get him."

If I didn't find a way into my dorm in the next minute it was all over. I could see the window of my room hiding in the bush. However, there would be at least one night TAC hanging out in the center of the box just waiting to catch me run into a room. If they saw me run into a room, they'd know who I was.

I began to panic when I heard a whistling sound and I looked through the leaves of the bush and saw Brett sticking out of the window. He threw a line of wrapped sheets out the window.

After looking in all directions to see that there were no TACs or cops in the area, I scurried to the sheet grazing the cement. Without thinking, I launched onto the sheet, grabbing it tight. When I felt Brett had a good grip, I climbed up one story and into my room. Brett closed the windows behind me as the lights illuminated the campus.

I lay on the floor out of breath and grateful to be there. I looked up at Brett. "Thanks a lot, man. You saved my ass."

"Yeah, and you're a pain in my ass, Rock. You're lucky that fat night TAC running outside the window woke me up talking on his radio."

"Dude, I owe you so much."

"Yeah you do. We better get into bed before they walk by and see us awake and realize it was you. Not to mention we have a game tomorrow."

We both crawled into our separate bunks and Brett fell asleep right way. I couldn't sleep. All I kept thinking about was how stupid I was to risk everything once again. I kept replaying the night over and over in my head until I heard the morning bugle sound off in the distance. Why did I keep doing everything to destroy any chance of succeeding in life? When would I learn that I had to pay my dues or I'd be a loser forever like the guy in the bus station?

The next morning, I hobbled out of bed not nearly as tired as I was anxious. Normally on game day I would be locked in all day, focusing on my job and mentally preparing for what

I needed to do come kickoff time. This time was different because for the first time in my life I would not be leading the team onto the field. Last year's team here had gone all the way to the semifinals and there was a lot of hype with the start of season. Many of the polls throughout New Mexico predicted that Hagerman was a clear-cut top three team at the 3A level.

The Hagerman football team had a lot of talent, speed, and size on the offensive side and was considered to be the largest and most experienced in our division. Our front five consisted entirely of seniors. Our two tackles were massive, with Borris Dawn manning the blind side and DeMarcus Everett at the right tackle. The two Sanford twins, Kyle and Richie were the starting guards for the team. They were both southern Texas guys, who weren't the sharpest tools in the shed, but were both strong as a couple oxen. Our skilled positions were mostly new guys with Donte Benson, the starting running back, Arturo Gomez, the starting tight end, and Brett, all being first year cadets

It felt strange not being a part of the starting team, yet I'd come to accept that if this is what coach felt was best then I would stand by his decision.

The game was an away game in Ruidoso, about an hour and a half west of Roswell. When the bus pulled into the stadium parking lot, Coach Lou stood in front of us. "All right, men, everyone knows their responsibility. Just be sure to take care of your job and we will get out of here with a win."

It was apparent early on that the Ruidoso team was not all that good and did not pose much of a threat to beating us. Because I wasn't getting the start I would have be there for the other guys though, and let them know what I saw. If anyone was struggling out there I planned to help them out as best I could.

Standing on the field during warm ups, I realized I had never been to a quaint town like this in the middle of the mountains. It certainly wasn't a mecca for football.

As I watched their team come out of their locker room and onto the field, I could see why they were not projected to do so well this year. Their team was a small team and while I watched their skilled position players warm up they clearly lacked talent. They had a very cool stadium that was filled with parents and friends of the players but it was much quieter than I was used to. Heck it was the first game of the season and you'd think there'd be a lot more excitement in the air? But not here. This certainly wasn't Premium or even Roswell. A lot of our team's parents had made the drive to Ruidoso to come watch their sons play in the opening game. Of course, I didn't have anyone come to watch me, but that really didn't bother me all that much.

I shivered in the cold clear night as the ball was finally kicked off to start the game and our season. From that moment, it was obvious who the better team was.

Standing on the sideline, I watched Jimmy take total command of the offense. I could hear him command the offense from the line of scrimmage, directing the team and changing plays when necessary. Every time he snapped the ball he executed the play swiftly and efficiently. It was clear that he was a very polished quarterback.

When Jimmy would throw the ball he was an accurate passer within ten yards, but he did not have a lot of velocity behind the ball, which meant he probably could not throw an accurate deep pass. Nevertheless this was his team and he had total control.

From start to finish we just ran over Ruidoso. They did not pose any realistic threat to any phase of the game. Our offense was crisp, the defense was punishing, and special teams put us in a good position to succeed. I was pretty happy when the final whistle blew to end the game. It was starting to get cold and I really just wanted to get back into the bus, but I felt proud of the guys and how they had played to the win.

We all stepped on the bus and were heading back to Roswell. The rest of the team was pumped and I was just as excited as them. It felt good being part of the guys and I realized how nice it was not to have to carry a team and to just be a part of one.

On the following Monday, the team learned that the Hagerman week would be different from every other team in the state. Most teams received two bye weeks throughout the season, where they didn't have to play a game that weekend. Most bye weeks came later in the season but our bye week was the upcoming Friday. This was an intentional decision made by the Institute because of a tradition that took place on the third Friday of the first school month for RATs, who were scheduled to complete the confidence course, that was supposed to test our physical aptitude. They made a big fuss about it at Hagerman. We still went about practice like we normally did, preparing for next weekend's opponent, Dexter High. They too had a high-powered offense and we all figured that the game might turn into a shootout. That was something Coach Lou wanted to avoid so we were spending a lot of practice time with the defense.

The week's practice went well for me. I'd put a lot of effort in by running the second teams offense. I knew if one of the first teams' players went down, one of my own guys would have to step up. Hell, if Jimmy were to go down, I would be the clear-cut starter, so I prepared just as if I was starting. I ran every play efficiently and quickly when my second team was called to run a play. I even found myself imitating some of Jimmy's leadership characteristics by helping some of the guys who were struggling with their individual jobs within the plays. If I noticed someone messing up, I approached them when the first or third team was running a play, and explained what they needed to do on that particular play. This helped me memorize my own job as well as learn the jobs of the other positions.

Jimmy, Brady, the sophomore third string quarterback, and I, spent large amounts of time together in the film room going over the opposition's defensive schemes throughout the week during our lunch period. I got to know Jimmy as a person, and realized that he was a pretty decent guy. He didn't have the same serious demeanor off the field, when he was hanging out with us in the locker room, as he did when he stepped onto the field. The week of film studying and practices helped the time pass, but in the back of my mind I knew the confidence course was close.

I was worried for Beal, that she would not be able to complete the running portion of the confidence course.

One morning I met Beal as Brett and I were out together. She bit her lip. "I'm never going make it, Rocky."

"Lets go out there and workout together. I can help you." We'd become good friends and she felt like the little sister I never had. She was the only person I confided to about Karen.

Completing the confidence course was extremely important

for us RATs. In order to obtain the privilege of going off campus we needed to pass their requirements, which included the obstacle course and one mile run.

We all got how important it was to obtain that privilege, and it was something that no one else could understand. We knew that we needed that break from being on campus, and if she could not get that break, she herself, was going to break.

Friday afternoon, as I sat in the back row of my class, I texted Karen underneath the desk telling her how worried I was for my friend. She was trying to comfort me saying that almost everyone gets through it. I knew she was only trying to comfort me, but deep down I knew Beal was in serious trouble.

The bell rang and I swung my bag over my shoulder and jogged to the box to change into my BDU's and get ready for the confidence course. Bret was getting dressed himself when I entered the room.

"I'm scared for poor Beal," I said.

Brett pulled on his shirt. "Don't worry, dude, she'll make it."

I struggled to get ready, distracted from thinking about what would happen if Beal did not pass. I heard a lot of rumors about those who don't pass the confidence course and how many of them quit the Institute soon after, because they can't handle life here without the off campus privilege.

"Left, left, left, right, left…" Archie kept calling as we all marched in step to his cadence. After we had crossed the bridge over Main Street, I began to look around to see if I could find the obstacle course. The pavement soon turned into dirt and rocks and I knew we were getting close. Off in the distance I saw military obstacles that stood in the way of a dirt path that I assumed we needed to get through. At the finish line, Golf Company was just completing the obstacle course. Many of the old cadets in charge of Golf Company stood around the group of RATs who had just finished. Some of them were exhausted and were sitting down on the ground. Others were exhilarated by the experience. All of them were covered head to toe with dirt. They had finished the course and the Company leaders were trying to organize them to head to the mile run.

When Golf Company had cleared the area, three cadets, also in BDU's, walked towards us from the course. One of them stood in front of us and explained how the obstacle course was going to work. I tuned him out for most of what he said. It was pretty self explanatory that we needed to get from point A to point B as fast as we could, and that there would be a bunch of obstacles in the way. When the cadet mentioned injuries I started to listen, because that was something I wanted to avoid happening to me.

"Again, the most important part of this challenge is your safety. Some of the obstacles are dangerous and require you to climb, jump, and crawl. You will be rolling around in the dirt and subjecting yourself to injury. We have had a few injuries already today, one of which was actually a member of our team, displaying how to jump over the seven-foot wall and landing with correct form."

I noticed First Sergeant Archie's face paled, as if he knew whom the person was who got hurt.

We all broke from formation and stood in front of the starting point for the obstacle course. Beal's face was white as a ghost as she stood next to me. I bumped her arm to get her attention and whispered, "Stay with me, I'll look after you."

She nodded her head and stared off into the course. My goal was going to be to help her get through this with exhausting the least amount of energy. That way she will have more strength to finish the mile. To the right of me, away from all of us RATs was First Sergeant Archie. He was talking to one of the course instructors and he still had a look of intense worry across his face. I was curious to what was bothering him, but I had to concentrate on getting Beal through this first.

The whistle blew and the company raced down the dirt path leading to the first obstacle. To the side of us was our entire Cadre, including my squad leader, Sergeant McCann. They cheered for us to get through this, yelling inspirational words. It was the first time they were trying to uplift us instead of yelling at us for doing something wrong.

"You guys are going to kick the shit out of this course," yelled a Platoon Leader.

"You guys are the best company in this core," shouted one of the squad leaders.

It really encouraged me not to let them down. Of course, Torrez was still trying to sabotage our effort, but we all ignored the guy.

The first course involved two long ropes that hung about thirty feet in the air from a steal beam. The course manager yelled, "Two of you up the rope at a time, the rest of you start running in place." We all ran in place but no one volunteered to be the first up the rope, so I took two steps to the rope, squatted down, and jumped up it as high as I could, wrapping my feet around the rope and clenching it with my hands above my head.

I had jumped almost a quarter of the way up the rope when

I looked up and started to climb. Brett followed with the same strategy to jump up it as high as he could. As I climbed further up the rope it caused it to sway back and forth. I had to use my core to stabilize the rope while climbing, managed to smack the top of the beam and began to climb down. When I hit the ground, I told Beal to go next and handed her the rope. She looked terrified. "It will be over soon. Don't worry. Just do it. I'm here for you."

She grabbed the rope and hopped a foot off the ground and hung on the rope. "Wrap your feet around the rope, like I did to stabilize yourself, and use your arms to pull yourself up," I said.

She did as I said and made her way up the rope. I stood beneath her knowing that if she fell, she would land on her back and injure herself. When she was about half way up, the rope started to sway as it had for me. This freaked her out and she stopped climbing. I could see the skin on her hands turn red as she squeezed the rope as tight as she could. Her breathing grew louder and quicker making it obvious that she was beginning to panic.

"I can't go any further," she cried.

I got on my knees and took hold of the rope with both hands and pulled down to the ground as hard as I could, stabilizing the rope for her. When the rope no longer swayed, she continued to climb without the threat of a swinging rope. Another one of the big guys in our Company did the same with the second rope, holding it stable for another girl climbing upwards. After she climbed down, I continued to hold the rope stable for others to climb up. I did so for about ten other RATs until Brett told me he would take over holding the rope stable.

When all of us had finished taking turns climbing up the rope, we headed to the next obstacle. With each upcoming obstacle I had a different idea on how to get through it. Some of the obstacles were harder than others but we all managed to find a way to get through them together. My plan with Beal was working really well so far, and that was what was most important to me. I was taking a lot of physical stress off of her and she still looked like she had a lot of energy in the tank left, which was going to be important after we finished with this course. I was concerned about her jumping that wall and landing without getting hurt.

I managed to get through with little trouble. My favorite obstacle was probably when we had to military crawl underneath the barbed wire. I felt like one of those guys in those badass war movies who have to go through some kind of boot camp and turn out to be a war hero.

As a company we managed to complete the course in the least amount of time of all the other companies that day. We all stood at the finish line covered head to toe in dirt, but unlike them none of us were on the ground exhausted. We were all standing, and exhilarated by what had just managed to accomplish. "She made it man," Brett said, thrilled Beal had gotten through the damn thing.

Beal beamed with excitement.

There wasn't a large portion of time allotted for celebration because soon after we had finished, our cadre was gathering us into formation and getting us ready for the mile long run. The excitement of the obstacle course quickly left me and I remembered the real reason why I was worried for my close friend. She had never completed the mile with our company much less complete it at a timed pace. This was the first time I had been nervous for someone else. I could only imagine what was going through Beal's mind.

We marched up to the starting point of our mile run and standing there was the Regimental Commander, Colonel Alex Adams. He was there with two of his regimental staff, holding a clipboard and pen. Our Company Commander saluted the Regimental Commander as we marched up to him. The RC told us to stand at ease and to listen up. "Congratulations on completing the obstacle course," he said, "this part of the confidence course is the mile run. You all will need to complete the run in less than thirteen minutes. I'm sure you all have been made aware of what will happen if you do not complete the run in the allotted amount of time. I have the utmost confidence that every one of you will complete the run here today, now please step up to the line and let's get started."

We made our way to the starting point and gathered into a formation, like we had done for our morning runs. I stood at the front of the company and looked back for Beal, but couldn't see her. Then the RC blew a whistle and we were off. The pace was nice and easy for me. We all stayed in formation and ran in step. "Look at what they have done to us," the fat, troublemaker, Brogan Davis said. "We are so fucked up and programmed we can't even run without being in step."

Most of the company laughed except for me since my mind was elsewhere. Brett noticed I was worried at about the half way mark. "You good?" he asked.

"Have you seen Beal?"

"Not since the halfway mark, I don't think she fell out though."

As I was about to take comfort in the fact that he said he had not seen her fall out. I noticed a young girl start to fall behind the company. I even heard people towards the back of the company yell, "Come on Beal, you are so close, don't quit."

"Rock," Brett said, knowing what I was thinking, "Take care of yourself first. You can't help her if you don't finish first. Do not fall out," he said.

Being in the front I began to pick up the pace of the run. The three others at the head of the formation running next to me maintained my pace, knowing that I wanted to finish this run, with everyone as fast as possible, to see what was going to happen to Beal. Everyone, but Beal, finished the run in ten minutes, though a lot of the young RATs were not thrilled that I picked up the pace towards the end.

Once we all crossed the finish line I tried to get a better view of where Beal was at and saw her at the three quarters mark. I could tell she was dying. She would start running, trying to motivate herself to keep going, and then she would stop to catch her breath and try and run again. The three quarters mark was the furthest she had ever gone and with two minutes and thirty-seconds left I really felt like she could finish the run if she could just find one last sliver of motivation.

"Move your ass, Beal," Torrez was yelling in her direction. "You are going to be the only one sitting in your dorm while all of your other little RAT buddies are running around the city." He had his arms folded and had a smirk on his face as if he was stoked that this poor girl was about to fail the run test. Torrez then turned around to another squad leader. "Twenty bucks says that dumb bitch doesn't even finish the run."

That was it. I turned around and got right in Torrez's face.

"Shut the fuck up."

His face was on fire. "What did you just say to me?"

"I am so tired of your shit and I am two-seconds away from beating your ass if you say one more thing about or to that girl."

Archie suddenly appeared with one of the platoon leaders and separated us. "What the hell is going on here," the RC asked.

I eyeballed Torrez. "Why don't you tell about your little bet with your buddy."

Torrez knew that if the RC heard what he had just said he would be in trouble so he said, "Nothing, sir, it's nothing."

"It better be nothing," the RC said walking away.

I stomped away from him and stared in Beal's direction. She had not traveled very far and was crunched over trying to catch her breath. She desperately wanted to finish the run and was doing everything in her power to complete it. Every Rat and every cadre member, except Torrez was yelling from the finish line trying to motivate her. Archie came up behind me and put his hand on my shoulder. "I just talked to the RC. He wanted me to tell you that you have permission to go out there and try and get her through this. You have a little less than two minutes so you better move your ass."

I sprinted out to Beal who had still not moved and was hunched over. When I reached Beal, she was having trouble taking deep breaths and there were tears streaming down her face. "Beal, you have less than two minutes to finish up."

"I can't do this, Rocky," she said with tears streaming down her face.

"Don't you dare quit on me," I told her in a firm voice.

"Don't worry about me anymore, maybe it's time for me to go."

"The only place you are going after this run is with Brett, Davey, and I off campus after this. Do you understand me?"

"I can't, I can't get through this, Rock."

"Yes, you can dammit. I am tired of seeing you feel sorry for yourself. You are too good to for that. There is something deep within you that we all have yet to see. You have a fire in you and I am going to bring that out of you so help me God."

"Rocky…"

"Be quiet," I interrupted still using a firm tone. "No more talking, start moving," I said.

She looked up from her hunched over position and her eyes sparkled when she noticed the rest of our company cheering for her. All of a sudden she stood tall slowly jogged. The tears were replaced with a powerful grin that had more motivation than I had ever seen in a person in all of my life. Her slow jog picked up speed with every step she took, she ran faster and faster until the girl was in a complete sprint.

Time was running out and First Sergeant Archie signaled me to hurry up. There had to be less than a minute. "Thirty-seconds," I told Beal, not taking any chances with how much time was left. Her speed increased even more to the point where I was in a dead run to keep up with her. "RUN!" I kept yelling, "Finish it, Beal. Finish it!" She ran through the core still cheering her on and crossed over that finish line, falling to her knees on the ground.

I raced up to her, going down to my knees, wrapping her in my arms. "You did it," I whispered in her ear. "I am so proud of you." She was so exhausted from that last burst of energy, that

I could hear her breathing through all of the cheers from all of the other RATS and Cadre in our company.

First Sergeant Archie threw a fist pump off to the side after he took a look at the RC's stopwatch. A massive weight was lifted off of my shoulders when I was sure she had beaten the thirteen-minute mark. He made his way through the company, standing around her cheering. He then bent over and put his arms on Beal's shoulders and stood her straight up. This massive man looked this young girl in the eye and told her loud enough for all of us to hear. "Remember the feeling you felt out there hunched over, thinking that you weren't going to finish the run, thinking that you were done here. Remember it for as long as you live because when that happens to you again and everyone around you is telling you, you can't do something, look them straight in the eye and you do what you just did here today. You say fuck that, and you run over anyone who gets in your way. Do you understand me Beal?" Archie asked.

She looked up at the massive Archie, and a tear strolled down her cheek. "Yes, First Sergeant."

"Don't forget you need to be back on post by ten tonight," he said with a wink then walked away.

She looked around at the crowd who had cheered her on. "Did I do it? Did I finish on time?" None of us really knew for sure although I assumed all was good. Just then Archie turned around and shouted, "Twelve minutes, fifty-two seconds."

The entire company cadre cheered again and took turns hugging her. A smile stretched ear to ear across her face.

Brett and I ran to our room and prepared to change into our Class C uniforms and meet up with Brogan and Beal to go off post for some real food. A knock on the door interrupted us as we were finishing getting dressed.

Brett headed to the door as I buttoned the last button on my uniform.

I heard Brett whispering to someone.

A minute later he closed the door and faced me. "First Sergeant wants to talk to you." He reopened the door and Archie stepped into our room. I assumed I was in big trouble for cussing out Torrez. While I knew Archie didn't like Torrez all that much, the fact was Torrez was an old cadet and I was a RAT. It was against the rules for a RAT to cuss out an old cadet.

"You guys going to get some dinner, Montoya," Archie said.

"Yes, First Sergeant," I replied, buttoning up my Class C.

Archie took off his First Sergeant hat. "Before you go, there is something you need to know, Montoya." He closed the door. "You are now the starting quarterback for the Hagerman Colts."

CHAPTER ELEVEN

I stood in the middle of my room staring at Archie in complete shock. "I'm sorry, what did you just say?"

Brett had stopped getting dressed and looked at Archie.

Archie looked solemn. "There was an accident today."

"What kind of an accident?" Brett asked.

Archie looked around the room having trouble maintaining eye contact. "Do you remember today when you were getting ready for the obstacle course, and one of the course leaders told you that one of them had gotten hurt trying to show a company how to land from a seven foot drop with good form?"

"Yeah," I said.

"That course instructor was Jimmy," Archie said.

"Bullshit," I said.

"Its true, I wouldn't joke around about something like that."

Brett asked, "Is he badly hurt?"

"It's bad. I went over to the infirmary after the mile run to see what had happened. Apparently he landed wrong and his knee buckled underneath his weight. They took him to Roswell Medical Hospital. They still need to do an MRI to check and see if there is any structural damage, but what I saw looked pretty bad. He couldn't put any pressure on it whatsoever."

"If he can't walk, that means he can't play next Friday against Dexter," Brett said.

"Exactly," Archie said looking at me, "I just felt that you had a right to know what was going on. If he can't play, Rocky, the job is yours. From what I saw today, you're ready to lead this team."

I stared back at Archie wide-eyed, not sure why I felt so strange. I had led teams onto the football field before. It wasn't like this Friday was going to be my first time being on the football field. But the fact that I'd be leading this group of men that were looking towards me for leadership, when I was the one who looked at within the core to lead me, scared the crap out of me. I stood up at attention. "Thanks, First Sergeant. I won't disappoint you."

Archie walked through the door threshold. "I know that. Now you guys make sure to get back on post by ten. And keep an eye out for Beal. Roswell isn't the safest place on earth."

Even though it was my first time off post with my friends all I could think about was getting to the locker room the next day to begin my preparations as starting quarterback. A part of me felt awful for Jimmy's accident, but another part could not help but feel excited for an opportunity to lead this team. It had been close to two months since I first stepped foot on this campus and I felt like in such a short period of time I have changed for the better, and I was excited to see how that change may have also transitioned onto the football field as well. I made a vow to work harder than I had ever worked in the past.

If I was not sneaking around to spend time with Karen,

I would be at practice, in school, or watching film of the upcoming opponent. My goal was to recognize the defensive play based on the formation of every team we would play.

Excitement in anticipation for next Friday's game had built in the pit of my stomach. I texted Karen throughout the night telling her the news.

"I'll be rooting for you every minute," she texted back.

I snuck the phone under the covers at night and we talked for hours in detail about how I planned to win the game. It thrilled me that she was so engaged with a topic that was so important to me.

The next day during the team meeting the coaches confirmed that I would be the starting quarterback on Friday against Dexter. Apparently Jimmy had completely blown out his knee when he landed, tearing his ACL. The doctors informed the coaches that tearing his ACL would put Jimmy out of any sort of real physical activity for 8-12 months. That meant I would be leading the football team this season.

When the team meeting ended, Coach Lou wiped some moisture from his eyes with a tissue. I knew how much he liked Jimmy and I also understood he didn't have that much confidence in me as his replacement. He had high hopes of winning this year, and he obviously felt the chances were now slim.

He didn't think I had what it took to win a big game for this team and I hadn't done anything to change that line of thinking. I already had a reputation for folding under pressure when things didn't naturally come easy for me. My new goal would be to prove him wrong once I was in the position with the pressure on me. I would lead the team under the pressure and succeed when everyone was looking at me to make the tough calls and plays.

After the meeting had concluded, I stayed behind in the locker room. There was no supper formation that night because it was Saturday so I took the opportunity to further look into Dexter's defensive schemes. Coach Castro remained with me two hours after everyone had left. I hoped he saw the effort and dedication I'd been putting in. He knew I had the ability. He wasn't interested in what I would do when everything was going right. What he wanted, was for me was to show him how I would play when everything went wrong.

As we got up to call it a night, Coach Castro touched my arm. "You've been blessed with an incredible gift. I have never coached anyone with the type of arm you have. Your footwork and mechanics are flawless and you have shown incredible mental discipline these last two weeks watching the film. You are ready and you are prepared. Now you must execute. Some people may not have faith that you can lead men on the field that lead you on a daily basis. It's a tricky business doing that, but make no mistake you are the General the moment you step onto that field. There will be twenty eyes looking at you to lead them into battle. Remember something kid, anyone can be confident and take charge when it's easy for them and when they are kicking ass out there. It's when times get tough on that field and things start to fall apart, and make no mistake, there will be times when the game plan goes to hell and you will have to find a way to win. Those are the times when a player and a man are truly defined. What I am trying to say is that I believe you are ready, and I have faith that you can do this."

As I walked back to my dorm, I kept on repeating Coach

Castro's words over and over again in my head. I will be defined based on how I act when times get hard. Throughout the night, I focused on this, and during study hall I memorized the playbook.

Brett had gone to the library so I kept going over the plays without any distractions. I could easily position myself looking at the book from my desk so that Company Officers, walking around making sure that we were studying, could not see that I was reading the playbook instead of my school textbooks.

After an hour and a half, the bugle sounded for a fifteen-minute break. Seconds later there was a knock on the door. I thought it was a Company Officer and threw the playbook to the back of my desk and pulled out my history book opening it to a random page before getting up to answer the door. I opened the door slowly. Suddenly I was pushed back propelling me backwards. Karen stepped into my room and quickly closed the door behind her. She wrapped her arms around the back of my neck kissing me where I stood. Now this was something that we could definitely get into deep shit for.

Not only was this fraternizing, but females were not allowed in our rooms with the doors closed. Despite knowing this, I was so excited that I didn't really care about the rules in this moment and I knew for a fact her crazy ass did not give a shit either.

We stood there kissing a while before she pulled back to look at me with the biggest smile. "I just thought you needed a good luck kiss before tomorrow's game, and I did not know if I would have another chance."

I smiled back at her. "Well, you definitely thought right."

"I missed you today."

"I just saw you last night," I said still holding her in my arms against the wall so no one walking by could see us.

"I know, but I just like being around you. You make me happy and when you aren't around I to miss you."

"Well, I missed you more."

"That's not possible."

"I'm really excited to see you in a cheerleader outfit tomorrow," I said looking her up and down.

"Better not let that distract you, Rock," she said kissing me again. "Probably shouldn't stay long either. I'd hate to ruin our streak of not getting caught. But before I go, I have a question for you. I told my girlfriend back in Albuquerque about you, and I kinda told her that you were my boyfriend. Is that all right with you?"

My answer was to kiss her again, then smile. "What do you think?"

"Good. I'll see you on the field Mr. Quarterback. Good luck tomorrow, I will be cheering for you."

I kissed her one last time and she snuck out of the room. She was gone as quickly as she had arrived. I went to sit down with a smile still plastered on my face. I was really excited that she wanted to be with me and with no one else. That fact may have distracted me from studying the playbook, but if anything it was a very worthy distraction.

I sat back down after closing the door and I couldn't get that beautiful girl out of my mind. The way she made me feel when I was with her and when I was away for her. I had never felt such a feeling like this about anyone. Hmmm, was this what love felt like?

CHAPTER TWELVE

I sat in front of my locker with headphones in my ears while the guys around me did their own thing to get into the zone. We had just returned from the field where we had finished our warm ups in preparation for the game. A thousand thoughts ran through my mind and my hands dripped wet with sweat. I closed my eyes and pictured each play unfold. Then I pictured defensive formations that I had memorized throughout the week, while watching film. I ran through everything twice before realizing that I was prepared.

People ascended into the stands. Some of the older football players had fear on their faces keenly aware that this game would be no easy task, unlike Ruidoso High School. Dexter was a different team that was especially known for their physicality and brutality. They had a huge offensive line and they loved to pound the ball on the ground. By watching the film I learned that they were a highly aggressive team who liked to jam receivers at the line of scrimmage and frequently send their linebackers in to blitz the quarterback, creating pass pressure. If we did not come out with our heads on straight, it was very possible for us to lose this game. I could see a couple of guys biting their fingernails as they looked over plays, while others listened to music shaking a knee.

Coach Lou walked into the locker room. "Five minutes, gentleman."

A part of me wanted to see what was currently going on at the football field, instead of waiting in the locker room. Apparently, when the away team finished warm ups they had to remain on the field at their sideline. When they concluded, the entire core marched to the field from the box. They made their way to the center of the field and were brought to attention. Then the national anthem played by HQ Company. When HQ was done, the entire core rushed to the stands behind our bench where they went ballistic, waiting for the start of the game. Many of the cadets were jumping in the stands creating a defining banging sound. Others were shouting as loud as they could in unison.

When I felt it was time, I stood and grabbed my helmet by the facemask. I walked from my locker with my chinstrap undone positioned in front of my mouth and looked down at my jersey, through my helmet's visor. The white colors shown brightly, with a cool dark black outline around my number and the team's name across the front of my chest.

As I peered at my number, the number two, I became even more excited for what was in store for me. Brett, who stood next to me, got up after I rose from the bench. Others also stood and were looking at me. I nodded at Archie who stood across the locker room. Then I moved toward the door with the entire team following close behind me.

We entered the locker room hall with our helmets perched on our heads. It was incredible how different the feeling and the degree of seriousness was that surrounded this team tonight. We proceeded to walk to the doors, which opened for us and we stopped. There were two lines of officers about ten yards apart. Each officer had his saber drawn and held up, almost as if to salute us. At the end of the line of these thirty officers was the cheerleading squad holding up a massive banner for us to run through.

Through all of that fanfare, I noticed Jimmy standing on crutches at the front of the right line of officers. I knew how badly he wanted this and how he must have wished he was in my shoes. Hell, he deserved to be in my shoes. If it hadn't been for that freak accident he would have been.

I turned around to face the entire team who was pumped up to break from the locker room jumping and yelling. I walked into the center of the team and held my right hand up high in the air in a fist. Those around me reached for my hand and those further out either just held their hand up in our direction, or on the shoulder pads of the guy in front of them. I stood there for a second, with everyone looking at me. "This one's for Jimmy. Our time on three: one, two, three. ..."

The entire team then shouted as loud as they could, "OUR TIME!" and then I broke into a dead sprint through the team, which opened a path for me through the doors and through the officers holding their sabers. I sensed the entire team behind me and once I broke through that banner and onto the field I got to see Colt Field completely lit up for a football game for the first time.

The stands behind our bench were full of Hagerman cadets who were going insane. The entire core was dressed in their BDU's, which created a sea of camouflage green in the stands.

The opposing benches were also filled with people, half with Dexter family members and the other half with the families of Hagerman cadets. A lot of people from Roswell had even come out and were standing around the field, because the stands and been completely filled. It was awe inspiring to see people from the community come out to support the team.

The noise from the screams was deafening as I ran down the center of the football field to our bench where the coaches stood. The guys were still jacked up standing on the sideline as our three captains, including Archie, walked to midfield to meet the referees and flip the coin to determine who would have possession of the ball in the first half.

I was standing on the sideline when I heard Beal and Brogan yelling from behind me in the stands. I turned to them and did a little chest pump to get them energized.

Brett did the same then stood beside me. "Ever see anything like this?"

I stared at the crowd behind us. "Not for a high school football game, man."

"You ready?"

I glanced at him for a second and smiled. "Let's find out."

Coach Lou yelled down the sideline. "Return team, get out there. Offense get ready!"

Brett held out a fist to me. I pumped it with mine as the ball had been kicked off to our return man. When he got tackled Brett looked at me with a smirk. "Let's just see how good you really are, Texan."

We ran onto the field along with nine other guys to start the opening drive for the game. Then we broke the huddle and lined up in a strong left power formation.

"Ready, set, go!" I commanded and the ball was snapped to me. Just as I handed the ball off to Donte he was immediately hit from behind the line of scrimmage and brought down. He took a brutal hit by the opposition, being that he had little momentum going forward while the defense had a full head of steam. I helped him up. "Are you all right, man?"

"Yeah, just got the wind knocked out of me," he said.

We headed back into the huddle. I yelled, "Go!" as the ball was snapped back to me, I dropped back three steps looking at both Brett and Steve along the outside. Just as they made their cut I was smacked from behind and went down hard. I lay on the ground for a second. The guy hit me pretty hard but it was nothing I hadn't felt before. I popped up soon after.

In the first two plays, we had lost eight yards and were facing a 3rd and 18. I quickly realized that the defense was sending one of their outside linebackers, around the tackle, while bringing one of their safeties up and having them blitz right up the A gap. This aggressive approach made it damn near impossible for us to get a run game going and it was also critical to for me to make quicker decisions.

I stepped to the line again and made the assumption the defense would line up conservatively since we had such a ways to go. But as I looked ahead at the defense, I saw one of the linebackers eyeing the gap that he was going to shoot through.

As I got into my snap position and commanded, "Ready," the outside cornerback left Brett and lined up on the line of scrimmage next to his defensive end. The safety came up and took the corner's position and stood over Brett. These cocky sons of bitches were showing me what they were going to do before the ball was even snapped.

I assumed I knew what was coming and would be able to get the ball off before going down. With little secondary coverage that meant one of my boys was going to have one-on-one coverage, which I always liked. As I snapped the ball, I learned it would be a lot harder than that.

One of the Sanford brothers picked up the blitzing linebacker. The left defensive end stunted downward through the gap that Richie had left wide open when he picked up the linebacker. Before I knew it the defensive end was right in my face. Brett had one-on-one coverage and he ran a fade route, sprinting straight down field. I threw the ball off my back foot straight up in the air as the defensive end hit me. I was lucky the ball was not intercepted thanks to Brett who managed to swat the poorly thrown ball out of the safeties hands, who had a clear path to the thrown ball.

Picking myself up from the ground I staggered to the sideline. The crowd was silent after that pathetic first three and out. I stood next to Coach Castro. "They're sending two guys every play and are trying to completely take the run away from us. I barely have time to react much less get the ball on target."

He clenched his jaw. "Are you able to read the play and know what's coming before you snap the ball?"

"I was able to for the first three plays."

"This is what I want you to do. Our boys are having trouble picking up the blitz, every time they show blitz I want you to audible to one of two plays, a quick screen to Donte or call for a double crossing slant route for Brett or Steven," Coach Castro said. "If the linebackers are blitzing up the middle then that will leave the middle of the field open for a quick slant route. Think to yourself, Rock, one, two, throw."

I glared at him. "One, two, throw?"

"Get the ball out of your hands in less than two-seconds."

I took a swig of water. "Gotcha, Coach."

The defense was having similar trouble as our offense was. Their offense was moving the ball easily on us, already crossing the fifty and into our territory with two big plays. The night had gone from a loud and vibrant one to a night of silence. The only noise that could be heard was Dexter players, as they grew more excited with each and every passing play. I became pissed off with my team and myself, mainly because these guys had dared come into our home and smack us around like we were nothing.

I walked up the sideline to where the lineman sat on the bench all together. Coach Tyson, the offensive line coach, had just gone over adjustments with them and they were clearly pissed off at the crappy job they had just done providing adequate protection. One of them had slammed his helmet on the ground while I could hear another cussing himself out underneath his breath.

I took a knee in front of them all, letting each of them get a good look at me. "I know coach probably already told you this but I need to get at least two more seconds from you. If you can get three full seconds then I promise you I can get this ball to move down field. This is what we are going to do. Every time we get to the line, I will give you guys a few seconds and I want each of you to call out a number before I call 'ready' ok? That number will be your man to block when I snap the ball, and that way no one will get confused again."

They agreed that if I gave them a few seconds at the line to figure out who specifically they would be blocking for that play, they could call out the numbers and make sure each of them know where they were going. The plan worked on the first play we ran when we took the field again. The defense was unable to stop Dexter's offense and they succeeded in driving the ball all the way down the field and then had run the ball in for a touchdown, putting us down by seven points.

The first play we ran, we ran for close to fifteen yards, to our 35-yard line. It was the first time I did not see a blitzing play, but that quickly changed when we lined up again for the second play. This time, all three linebackers were lining up right behind their defensive line, showing blitz the whole time. "91, 73, 51…" were being called by my offensive lineman, but there was going to be seven blitzing and that meant one defensive player was going to be coming at me unblocked.

"Check, Rio Grande. Check, Rio Grande!" I shouted at both of the receivers and line, signaling for both my receivers to run a quick slant route. I then took a few steps, lining up in a shotgun formation, with Donte now standing right next to me. "Ready, set, go!" I caught the ball and took one step back, planting my foot into the ground. I could see that Brett had a step on the corner while at the same time, one of the linebackers was barreling down on me. I brought the ball back and rifled it to where Brett was going to be. He managed to stretch out and bring it in for an eight-yard gain.

We kept that style of play up for the drive, checking to an audible whenever they showed a blitz of two or more defensive players. It took us eleven plays but we managed to get the ball down into the opposition's six-yard line. The first two plays were half back dives, giving the ball to Donte, to have him try and run it in, but both times he was stopped at the line of scrimmage. The defense had lined up in their goal line stance, with two linebackers dropping back to the middle of the field to watch for the quick slant pass.

On third down and goal, with six yards to go before we got into the end zone, we huddled for the incoming play. It was going to be a play action pass, faking the run to Donte and then rolling out to the side and looking to pass the ball to Brett, Steven, Arturo, or Donte. Before we broke the huddle, I looked at Brett. "Fake as if you are going to run a slant route to the middle and then cut back again to the outside."

He nodded.

I figured that the corners were going to play him as if he was going to run the inside slant and try and take the middle of the field away. If he cut in, pretending to run a slant route, they would jump the route and look to intercept the ball. When they jumped the route it would leave the outside wide open, and if he cut back while I rolled out in his direction, it would be nothing more then a six yard pass to a wide open receiver.

The plan worked. I snapped the ball and fake handed the ball to Donte, who was tackled at the line. Dexter was completely fooled as they thought Donte had the ball in his hands. I rolled out to my right but the defensive end on that side did not take the bait. He noticed immediately it was a play action and he broke off from the run and began to chase me, running less then a couple feet away from me. Slapping his reaching hand away from me, I looked up and Brett had just cut back to the outside. The corner had jumped the route and when Brett had cut back to the outside, the corner had slipped and fallen to the ground. There were no safeties or linebackers in that area of the field, so I floated the ball as the defensive end dove at my feet, bringing me to the ground. The ball softly landed into Brett's hands, successfully scoring a touchdown.

I pushed myself up from the ground, ran to Brett in the end zone and wrapped my arms around him along with the majority of the team. It had been my first touchdown pass in what seemed like an eternity. I probably had thrown a hundred touchdowns up to that point in my entire high school football career, but this one felt special.

That drive and touchdown brought the crowd back to life again, and the entire stands jumped and screamed like we had just won the Super Bowl. They pounded down on the steel bleachers so every jumping cadet made a loud echoing noise. With nearly a thousand doing it at the same time, the noise was deafening.

This atmosphere remained for the rest of the game, as our offensive successfully translated to the defensive side of the ball. The defense was now exhilarated and played a hell of a lot better than they did on that first drive of the game. We moved the ball on the offensive side almost every time we touched it. I read their defense as if I were reading a book. I recognized the majority of their plays based on their defensive positioning and the situation in the game. I knew what was coming before I even snapped the ball, which made it all that much easier for me.

For the first half of the game, we threw the ball all over the field. Their aggressive defensive style allowed for a significant amount of wide-open space in the secondary. Our line, calling out the numbers to blitzing players, provided me a lot more time to sit in the pocket and make a decision with the ball. In the first half, I threw for over 200 yards and two touchdowns.

What really ended up killing Dexter was when they realized I was able to read their plays. So they deviated from their game plan midway through the second quarter. They began to drop their linebackers into zone protection, no longer blitzing them anymore. This change of now having only four defensive linemen to defend against my line, successfully gave me not just the three-seconds that I asked for, but upwards of five or six-seconds. This allowed more than enough time for me to decide where I was going to throw the ball.

The conservative defensive play calls not only allowed for me to run it, if no one was open, but also created holes that a semi truck could drive through for Donte. By the end of the game, he ran for well over a hundred yards and also succeeded in securing a touchdown. I threw for a few yards over 300 and tacked on a second half touchdown pass. We ended up blowing out Dexter 31-10 when the final whistle blew.

The core had the same amount of energy as it did when we came onto the field as it did when we left the field. We were all jacked to have beaten down a team like Dexter that was supposed to present a challenge for us.

I sat in my locker smiling, thinking for the first time how happy I was to be back in uniform with these pads, and these guys. I had not realized what I had with football until it was taken from me. Now that I had it back, I was not going to lose it again.

CHAPTER THIRTEEN

A few weeks had passed since the Dexter game, and we had won three games since then. This put us at a record of 5-0, and we had garnered recognition across the state as one of the best teams in the state. Hagerman was being seen as a team that had a real chance at taking home the State Championship. The team was rolling and we had established a true identity.

Prior to the start of the season, we were a running team. However, the coaches ultimately decided to move away from that and switched to a pass first philosophy. So far it had really worked and in the four games we'd played, I had thrown for sixteen touchdowns with only a single interception. Scouts began to take notice of my stats and showed up unannounced at our games. I assumed a large portion of them still thought of me as a bit of a loose cannon and feared that I could lose it at any time. However, I allowed myself to believe that few scouts might think I had matured since they had last spoken to me.

After Friday's victory, a scout from the University of Louisville showed up outside the locker room and invited me to get coffee with him. After I changed, he and I went over to the PX where we sat at a small table. The scout, a short bald guy with a handlebar mustache, ordered the coffee. "I'm impressed how you've learned to take charge out there, son."

I sipped the coffee slowly then smiled at him. "Thank you, sir."

"I have been following your progression for the last two years and I am pleased to see how far you have come. Its quite impressive to see the change."

"This place will do that to you. I quickly learned that I better get with the program or I would be tossed out to the curb."

"I can see that. Would you say you're a changed person?"

"I wouldn't say I am a changed person but I would say I am a better version of myself. Hagerman is designed to break you down so they can mold you into the best person you can be, and that's what they did for me."

"What was that process like for you, son?" the old recruit asked.

"In a word, Grueling. I don't know how some of the other first year cadets did it because most of them are years younger than me. There's no denying it was tough for me. I came from a place where I could do no wrong to a place where I could do little right. It took a while for me, but I finally was able to adapt."

"When did you turn that corner?" he asked.

I paused for a moment thinking about the time when I was sitting at the bus stop ready to run away, and how different things would be if I ran away from my demons instead of face them. "I guess it was when I hit rock bottom. At that moment I was at a crossroads where I was going to make a decision that would affect the rest of my life. I chose the harder of the two routes. To answer your question though, I turned the corner when I finally accepted that Hagerman was now my home and that I was going to have to make the best of it."

"Well, Rocky, I am very pleased to see your development as both a football player and a young man and I can assure you that we will be keeping an eye on you. If things keep going the way they are going we will definably have a spot for you at Louisville."

"Thank you, sir."

These types of compliments were nice, but I knew that the scouts were going to be patient and wait for a game that involved a defense that truly frustrated me and made it difficult for our offense to move the ball. The best team we had faced had been Dexter in week two, but we had yet to face an elite team that challenged us with an elite defense. The teams that we had faced made it easy for me to pick apart their defense with complete ease, and move the ball almost at will.

Lovington High School, Hagerman's arch rival was on the schedule next. We had two weeks to prepare for this game, being that it was our second scheduled bye week. Lovington, too, had a bye week so there would be no advantage either way.

Throughout the week we were all on par with what we needed to get done that day in practice, both on the field and in the film room. It was the most efficient and intense week of practice that I had been a part of. When Friday night rolled around, I was thrilled to be able to take a break from football, since our game against Lovington was going to be played next week.

I sat in the locker room changing along side Brett when

Archie came up to us and asked what we were planning on doing after supper formation. "I'm going to try and get some studying done," I said lying. My real plan was to meet up with Karen and go somewhere in the city to spend some time together.

Brett nodded even though I'm sure he suspected I was bullshitting. He knew about Karen and I. While he did not agree with playing around with frat, he had my back.

"You guys got all weekend to study," Archie said. "You need to get ready for the formal inspection."

I glared at him. "Formal Inspection?"

"That's right. Remember when I told you about formal inspections the first week of matriculation?"

"Yeah," I said, lying. I had no recollection of what he was talking about.

"We don't have a game this Friday, so you guys, along with all of the other football players will be a part of the formal inspection and the parade."

"That's just great," I said. "When is the formal inspection?"

"Tomorrow morning. Goddamn it, guys, do you ever listen when I am talking to the company?"

"Sure do," Brett said covering his smile with his hand.

Archie gawked at us. "Get your room straight for the inspection. You have all night to get ready for it. Read the book we gave you at matriculation how to get ready for it."

"Will do," I said as Archie headed toward the locker rooms exit.

When he was gone, I turned to Brett. "I don't remember him talking about formal inspections so maybe you can fill in the holes for me."

"Jesus, Rock, what would you do without me?" he said. "The formal inspection is not like our daily inspections. We will be inspected by a member of regimental staff and they go through our entire room. We need to make sure everything is spotless. Our closet, mirrors, desks and everything else need to be organized a certain way. We'll have to stand at attention in our formal uniforms. They'll inspect our uniforms from head-to-toe. After that, we all have to form up for a parade at Stapp field."

"That sounds fucking awful," I said.

Brett shook his head. "One of my buddies told me about their first formal inspection, three weeks ago, and he said it sucks ass. It will take us a lot of the night to get ready and it's a three hour process, including the parade."

"We have to find a way to get out of it." I said.

"Don't even think about it, Rocky. We ditch the formal inspection they will stick us up the ass and we will be marching tours, for the rest of the year. We have to suck it up."

"Fuck me. Now I got to let Karen know I can't go off tonight."

I couldn't help thinking how one minute I felt grateful to be at Hagerman, and the next I hated the place.

CHAPTER FOURTEEN

That night, Brett and I spent hour after hour getting ready for the formal inspection. We found the inspection page that explained how to specifically prepare our room. The closet needed to be organized a certain way with all of our clothes cleaned, perfectly folded, and placed in a designated spot. Our sinks, mirrors, and desks also had to have the same type of detailed organization.

The majority of the core was in the same position as us and had waited for the last night to get their rooms ready for the formal inspection. People raced around through the box, borrowing cleaning supplies, vacuums, and air fresheners from their friends. It was not just RATs but old cadets doing the same things. It wasn't any fun getting ready for a formal inspection. Everyone's stress level was through the roof as they went about preparing their rooms.

The most stressed out individual was Brogan. He kept coming into our room asking to borrow stuff. The kid was beyond hysterical, because we all knew that he was going to get his ass kicked in the inspection. Even he knew it, but he still tried hard to get his room ready. "Come on guys, just let me get the vacuum for thirty minutes."

Brett stopped scrubbing the sink and looked at Brogan. "Thirty minutes? It ain't like we are staying at a penthouse in Vegas. These rooms are no bigger than a teenager's closet."

"Come on, I'm serious, these guys are going to go off on me."

"Fine, but bring it back at soon as you can. We would like to get some sleep tonight."

Brogan reached for the vacuum but before he left the room he said, "Can I snag a couple sheets of Lysol?"

"Do you have any cleaning supplies at all?" Brett asked.

"Don't be a dick," Brogan said.

"The Lysol is in the closet," I said pointing to where we kept the supplies.

Brogan picked up the vacuum. "By the way, we are all fucked for this inspection?"

I frowned. "Why is that?"

"You didn't hear who was inspecting us?"

"No," Brett said. "Who is it?"

"The fucking Regimental Commander."

"Bullshit."

"Why would I lie about something like that?"

"That sucks," I said. "You might as well just stop getting ready Brogan."

"Why's that?"

"Dude, you're his favorite RAT. He is probably so excited to see you tomorrow," I said laughing.

"You guys are dicks," he said. By his expression, it was obvious he realized that he was beyond screwed, no matter what he did.

It was the most cleaning I had ever done in my entire life. My mother had done all the housework when I was growing up so this type of head-to-toe cleaning was new to me.

When the clock finally struck midnight, Brett and I had finished getting our room ready. It was spotless like a first class hotel room. We had set up our formal uniforms. They hung from each of our closets ready to go for the morning.

"What a workout," Brett said as he tucked in.

I yawned. "More exercise than any practice I've been to."

It had felt like I'd just put my head down on the pillow when my alarm went off. I jumped out of bed to turn it off, praying that it had gone off early but the clock showed 6 am. A few seconds later, the bugle sounded loud and clear signaling a brand new day at Hagerman.

We did the usual morning formation, but the squad leaders didn't check our uniforms, knowing that we were going to change into our formal uniforms after breakfast. Before letting us file into the mess hall, First Sergeant Archie stood in front of the company. "You all have less than two hours from now to eat and get back to your rooms to make any last minute changes. Leave yourself enough time to make sure you have a clean shave and that your shoes and buckles are shining. I know it's been a pain in the ass but let's just get through this as quickly as we can."

Brett and I took our time with breakfast unlike a majority of the other RATs who hustled through the meal and rushed back to their rooms to get their uniforms ready. We eventually made our way to back to the room but the box was as busy as ever. With everyone stressed and racing around, it seemed like they were taking this formal inspection more seriously than

Brett and me. I figured it was because a lot of people had a high number of demerits and didn't have any room to afford more. Luckily, I had yet to be stuck for anything, alleviating my stress some.

I used the two hours to make final corrections on the room and to catch up on some sleep. I had no idea where Brett had gone so I turned off the lights and climbed into bed.

Just as I was dozing off, I heard a hard knock on the door. I opened it thinking Brett had forgotten his keys, but it was Karen not Brett who slid through the door and closed it behind her.

"What are you doing?" I said after she kissed me passionately.

"I missed you," she said in between kisses.

"Did anyone see you?"

"Of course not. I never get caught."

"You know if we get caught--"

"I know the risk, but I won't get caught. Now shut up," she said smiling and pulling me close to her again. Unlike the few times she had snuck into my room, this encounter was not a quick hello. To be honest, we did not stop at making out. We made our way into my bed, one thing led to another.

Thank God, all of the high ranking cadets were either getting ready to be doing the inspection or making sure specific cadets in their company were ready. Our Company Commander had come by the night before to assure us that we were ready, so I knew he was not going to walk by and notice the shade down. If anyone did notice, I would hear them banging my door.

The worry soon left my mind.

"What time does Brett come back?" she asked.

"Not for a while."

She responded with another kiss.

We made love for an hour without anyone disturbing us in my room. While it was the most risky thing I'd ever done, I'd do it again tomorrow. Forbidden love made it all the more exciting. We both did not care about the dire consequences as we held each other in our arms. It was the most amazing experience I'd had at Hagerman. I dare say, it was the best experience in my life so far. Judging by the smile on Karen's face, she felt the same as me.

Bam, bam, bam! My worst fear had become a reality. Someone banged the door. Based on the way they were knocking, I knew it was someone with rank. We were dead if they saw Karen in my room with proof that we had just had sex. They could prove sexual misconduct and give reason to kick us out of Hagerman. For me, it would be a one-way trip to jail. But it was Karen I worried about.

I jumped out of bed and helped Karen down. She was trembling so much she could hardly move. There was not a lot of time before the person knocking knew that something was not right.

I rushed Karen to the back of the room and she climbed into the closet. Then I shoved most of our clothes which were tossed all over the place, under the bed. I threw on some boxers, took a deep breath, and opened the door.

Captain O'Malley, Hotels Company Officer and former Marine, stood there with a puzzled expression on his ugly pockmarked face. He knew how to intimidate the hell out of people. One thing that he absolutely hated was when people kept their shades down. He glared at me. "Why is your shade down, cadet?"

"I'm sorry sir, I was taking a nap."

"You shouldn't be napping. You have an inspection in less than an hour."

"Yes, sir, I know. I am ready for it. Members of my cadre already checked my room out and said that both me and my roommate are good to go."

"I could stick you for having your shade down for an extended period of time, you know."

"Sir, I am sorry. I promise I won't keep my shade down for that long again. I was just trying to block out some sun. It will not happen again," I said.

"This is your one warning. Keep that shade up or else you will be marching tours. Do you understand me?"

"Yes, sir," I said. I turned and raised the shade as calmly as I could, hoping that the Captain would not think anything suspicious was going on. When I turned to look at him I stupidly glanced at the closed closet door where Karen was hiding.

"Something going on in here that's not supposed to be going on?" he asked.

"No, sir, we still have some more cleaning to do is all," I said. Then I saw Karen's bra straps sticking out from under the bed. Life as I knew it was about to end if I didn't act quickly.

I forced a loud sneeze and in the same motion, I moved my foot over the white bands of bra strap. I thought for sure he would notice.

O'Malley brushed his crew cut with the palm of his hand. "You're acting strange, cadet. I can't put my finger on it, but something is off with you."

All I could think about was what would happen to Karen.

Adversity was nothing new in my sorry life. Drops of sweat formed above my lip. If O'Malley observed the perspiration or looked beneath my big foot, Karen and I were done. But I managed a weak smile like I didn't have a care in the world. "No, sir. Just nervous for the big inspection."

He nodded and glanced around one more time. Then he shook his head and left the room. When he was out of sight, I picked up Karen's clothes from under the bed and handed them through the closet door to her. If we were caught in the room together dressed, it would at the most be a 10-20 stick. A hell of a lot better than a sexual misconduct.

As she dressed, Brett walked through the door. Can this really get any worse ?

Brett, of course, had no idea Karen was changing in the closet and he sat down in his chair. I looked outside to see if there was anyone on my stoop who would get me in trouble. I knew this was the window we needed to get her out without getting caught. I opened the closet door and she steeped out.

Brett shot straight up out of his chair, as I let her to the front door gave her a kiss. "I'll call you after the parade."

She smiled and scooted out of the room.

I then looked at Brett who still appeared stunned.

"Don't look at me like that, it's not a big deal," I said with a smirk.

"You're right," he snapped. "I'm sorry. Next time just leave a sock on the door and I will be sure to come back later."

"Come on, she was in and out, you don't need to get sarcastic."

"Dude, you can't just have her running in and out of our room like this is a frat house. These fuckers will crucify you if they realize that you are fraternizing with her, much less catching you guys fucking on post. If you are going to do that, go get a hotel like everyone else around here. "

"It wasn't my idea, she just showed up here and busted through," I said.

"I am just saying be careful. They really like to keep an eye out for that kind of stuff. It would be a bitch for you to get kicked out when you have come so far."

"I know. We actually almost did get caught. Captain O'Malley knocked on the door when he saw the shade down. I put Karen in the closet so we wouldn't get busted. Miraculously, he didn't notice her clothes on the floor or the fact I was sweating bullets."

"You're playing with fire and your ass is getting close to getting burned."

"You're right. I am going to have to cool it."

"Good," he said pausing for a moment and then grinning. "Dude, she is fucking hot."

I laughed. "Don't I know it."

The hour before the inspection soon passed and the bugle sounded, indicating that it was about to begin. Brett and I looked through the window and saw members of regimental walking to their assigned companies to formally inspect us. The Regimental Commander bypassed all of the other companies and headed straight through to our company area. Brogan wasn't bullshitting. The RC really was inspecting us.

The Colonel did not waste any time meeting our Company's officers, heading instead to the first room to inspect. When Brett and I saw this, we both stood in front of our desks, ready to come to attention when they entered our room. We had no idea how long it would take for them to get up to where we were on the second level.

An hour passed, and we grew bored with literally nothing to do but wait. It reached a point where we just wanted them to get to us so that we could get the damn thing over with. As I started to loosen my tie and relax a little, I heard the RC's voice down the stoop, on the second level. I cracked the door open and poked my head through to see how far down they where. Right when I poked my head out the door I saw First Sergeant and one of the platoon officers sauntered into a room two doors down from Brett me, and one door down from Brogan and his roommate.

I glanced at Brett. "Shit, they're almost here!"

"Geez. Lets check everything a last time," he said.

My heart raced wildly even though I knew we'd done a good job, a fucking fantastic job. Our uniforms were perfectly set up, the beds were finely made and everything was organized just the way the book instructed us.

"Oh my God, look at this!" Brett said as he opened a drawer on the side of his desk, which was supposed to be empty. His eyes bulged out like a bullfrog. He turned to me holding a large Papa John's pizza box from three days ago.

This whole day was about to be ruined because of a pizza box. The officers wouldn't even inspect us if they saw us standing with the damn thing. They'd just stick us. And it wasn't like we could hide it anywhere in the room.

Brett bolted to the door in an attempt to sneak to the garbage down the hall and toss it there. He pulled his head back in when he saw the RC walking to Brogans room. "We are totally fucked!" he said.

"Give me the box," I said grabbing it from his hands. I ran to the back window, pulled it open, and slung the pizza box out like a Frisbee. What happened next either defined me and Brett's luck, or Brogan's lack of luck when it came to the RC. The box flung out my window, rode upwards with the wind, then came around and flew back towards the building.

There were screams in the next room. Apparently, the pizza box flew through Brogan's window and landed right in the middle of the room.

"What the fuck!" Brogan shouted.

But that wasn't even the best part. As it had landed in the center of the room, the RC simultaneously turned the corner and entered the room. The screams from the RC could be heard several rooms down.

Brett and I laughed uncontrollably. You could do something like that a thousand times over and never replicate what had just happened.

We eventually composed ourselves. When we realized that the RC was probably on his way to our room seconds later, the RC entered our room holding a clipboard. He had a sneer on his face making it that much harder for Brett and me not lose control and start laughing again.

The RC examined our room carefully, checking things off on his clipboard and then exited soon after. He didn't spend more than two minutes in our room.

First Sergeant Archie followed the officers out of the room but turned back to us before exiting. "Formation is ten minutes for the parade don't go anywhere."

What bullshit. All of that preparation for a quick inspection was crazy. "What the hell, dude?" I said to Brett.

"What?"

"We stayed up all night getting ready and they barely even checked our room out. They didn't even check out our uniforms or anything. That's crap."

"Hey man, that happens sometimes," Brett said. He took his garrison cap off and sat down in his chair.

"I don't understand," I said.

"Maybe they got behind schedule or something. I mean they have two more rooms to check on this stoop. You heard Archie. We have to form up for the parade in ten minutes. What probably happened was the RC took too long with the first stoop and so had to check everyone else quickly."

"Man, I just don't get this school sometimes," I said. "They tell us to do all this work. And for what?"

"Dude, it's a military school. It's supposed to suck ass and piss you off."

"Sometimes I think that this school is just completely worthless and that there's no point to most of the shit we do on a daily basis."

Brett smiled. "I used to think the exact same thing when I first got here. I didn't understand why I was doing most of the shit they assigned us in the military schools I attended before this one. Then I went home for break and I began to understand."

"And what was your revelation?" I asked.

"It's too hard to explain, but you'll notice the difference when you see your friends from home. You will see how much more prepared you are for real life than they are. It's a strange thing, dude. You jump through these hoops, thinking they are pointless, but really they are teaching you discipline through action. My dad always said we all owe a debt the moment we are born, and that debt must be paid by all. Few pay now, most pay later, and you must decide to either pay now or pay later."

"What does that even mean?"

"By being here, you are paying now by working your ass off. Because of it, you will be successful one day, in whatever you do. Unlike others, who are partying and messing around now, they will have to pay later. What I'm trying to say is that there is a reason for this crap, you just need to trust in the process."

"I hope you are right, bud."

"Trust me. You will see one day, hell maybe ten years after you have left this place. You'll look back and be appreciative of all of this because it will be the reason you get where you want to go."

"Jesus, that's some deep shit, man."

"I know, sorry. I didn't get much sleep either," he said laughing. "I am going to go see if Brogan is still alive. Want to come?"

"Nah, I'm just going to hang around here until the parade."

"You all right?" Brett asked.

"Yeah, yeah I'm good. I'll see you out there soon."

I was lying to Brett.

CHAPTER FIFTEEN

The drums beat out from the field, maintaining a cadence for the cadets marching. The core was forming up and preparing for the national anthem in front of a crowed mixed with Lovington and Hagerman fans. In a few minutes they would start to go crazy and run for the stand behind our bench.

Donte told me earlier that when he looked out of the locker room doors that there were more people here to see a high school game than he had ever seen before. Apparently, the vast majority of Lovington had made the two-hour drive with the team earlier today to watch the game.

I drowned out the noise from outside as I thought about our strategy for the game. The second week of practice had not been as efficient as the first week, since a substantial amount of guys had gotten sick throughout the week and missed practice. Hell, we were fortunate enough to get everyone back in uniform tonight, much less make sure they were one-hundred percent prepared.

No one was talking as I sat by my locker. Everyone appeared to be zoning out. I hoped they were thinking about their responsibilities and jobs on the field. Their faces looked fearful especially those who missed practice this past week. The realization that we were not as prepared as our opponent made me fear we were heading into the lion's den.

I knew one thing for sure. They'd all be looking at me to carry them through. I had become their undisputed leader through my hard work in the film room with Coach Castro, at practice and in the games. The team had voted me to be one of the captains taking over Jimmy's spot. Tonight would be a true test as the leader of this group.

Coach Castro stood with us in the locker room with a somber expression on his face. "Five minutes, guys."

I placed my helmet over my head with the chinstrap over my mouth. Something needed to be said to these guys to calm them down. I moved to the center of the locker room and shouted. "Everyone, huddle around me."

They picked up their helmets and came to the center of the locker room and surrounding me.

I looked at each of them dead in the eye before opening my mouth. "No one thinks we will win this game. You all probably know The Roswell Daily has predicted we will lose by more than seventeen points. They assume we're going to get our asses kicked. People here at Hagerman may be excited but in the back of their minds they too think we have a slim shot at beating a team who is in a higher class than us."

I then eyeballed each of them before continuing. "If you think for one-second that any of them are right, I want you to put your helmet down, take your pads off, and leave this locker room, because it is total crap. Stare at them across the field and you show them no fear. The moment that ball is kicked to start the game you hit anyone not wearing a Colts jersey, and when you hit them, you knock them straight into tomorrow. Do not help a single one of their players up, do not congratulate them, do not show them weakness, because they will show you none." I paused to look into the eyes of every one of my teammates.

"Gentleman," I continued, "tonight we shall see what this team really is made of, and if you give me everything you have tonight, I swear to God we will march off this field victorious. Hands in boys."

Everyone held up their fists in unison.

"Let me hear you. Our time on three…one, two, three."

And with that, the locker room roared, "OUR TIME!" We then stormed toward the door where we stood waiting to run onto our field. When we busted through the paper wall held by the cheerleaders, I led the team to the center of the football field and to our sideline. Taking a swig of water, I noticed the entire team was doing what I said in that they all were staring across the field at Lovington's team.

It was cold night and every exhale was seen through each of our facemasks. The core behind us was loud as ever. They were doing all they could do to intimidate Lovington's football players, knowing that they too were a hell of a football team, a higher class than us and undefeated.

Coach Lou called for us captains to head out for the coin toss. Archie, the two Sanford brothers, and I stepped forward and marched to midfield to determine who would get the ball first. Four of Lovington's players had already paced in from their side of the field and their captains looked massive.

"Stare them straight in the eye when we get there and do not lose eye contact," I said to the other captains. As I stood at midfield listening to the referee's instructions about the coin toss, I found myself across from their star defensive end. He was much taller and broader than me, a massive individual, but I focused on my own words and never broke eye contact. Even though I was scared shitless about being blindsided by this guy, I refused to show him that. After this coin toss, I would to make sure he thought I was the most arrogant fuck he had ever stood across from on that football field.

"Tails," called one of their captains.

"Tails it is," the referee said looking at Lovington's captains.

"We will receive," their captains said.

I pointed east, telling the referee that we would defend that way.

"All right, gentlemen, shake hands," the referee said and then walked away.

As I shook hands with the defensive end who squeezed the hell out of my hand, he said, "I can't wait to knock your fucking teeth in, douche bag."

I grinned at him. "First you have to catch me, fat boy."

Words were shared between the other six players who simultaneously shook hands too. Clearly, this game would be a hell of a lot more intense than any other we had played this year. I had never been a part of a true hated rivalry before that night. This game would get very chippy, and there'd be a lot of extra activity after the whistle was blown. I had heard rumors that the referees had the reputation for letting the game play and not calling a significant amount of penalties.

"Get pissed off, Brett," I said, as the kick off team lined up. "It's going to be a hard hitting one, and something tells me these boys don't exactly abide by the rules."

From the moment the ball was kicked off, the tone of the game was set. People flew full speed down the field, every play, hitting their opponent with everything they had. Their boys were as pumped up for this game as we were. The game did, in fact, become chippy within the first few plays of our defense taking the field. Players on both teams pushed and shoved each other after each play and shouted and cussed. But that was always to be expected. The Lovington fans did their part screaming with every play run for their team. And the core was right behind us drowning them out.

From the sideline, I could hear every pop of the pads, with every hit. Our defense stood strong, eventually stopping Lovington's initial drive at midfield, forcing them to punt. I buckled my chinstrap, ready to enter into this rivalry. I knew there were a lot of scouts here to see me against this ferocious defense, but I didn't allow myself to worry about that. My mind was completely focused on what I needed to do for this team. Steve called a fair catch at our nineteen-yard-line once the ball was punted away, and our offense was sent to the field for the first time.

"Huddle up," Archie called.

"All right, boys, 34 half back draw, first sound," I said, followed by a break by the offense.

Eleven of us lined up in shotgun formation, and I waited to see how the defense was going to line up. After a moment, they began to show a blitz, looking like they were going to stunt the A gaps. That would force Donte right into the teeth of the defense. I decided to audible out of the play calling, "Check Peter Pan, check Peter Pan," making sure that everyone on the offense had heard the changed play.

While I was changing the play, the defense shouted at us from their positioning, in an attempt to block my offense from hearing the change of play. I remained focused storming up to the line and yelling, "52 is the Mike, 52 is the Mike." I then took a few steps back into position next to Donte, with only a few seconds before a delay of game penalty and snapped the ball. I dropped back three steps, planted my back foot into the ground and zipped the ball right into Brett's chest, who was running a hook route, ten yards deep. He was immediately tackled after catching the ball, gaining ten yards, and subsequently moving the chains.

We huddled again and called a running play. The defense this time was backed up, not showing blitz, but they were still mouthing off. We ran the ball off tackle and Donte raced right around their stud defense end, who Borris was handling quite well at this point. The defense end did manage to get a hand onto Donte's jersey, but Donte shoved him off and ended up picking up a nice gain of twelve yards. Like every other play, there was shoving after the whistle. Brett was getting into it with the corner on him, but no one was talking more shit between each other than Archie and the nose tackle he was lined up against.

Coach Lou must have liked what he saw because he told us to run the ball again, and again it worked. This time Donte ended up running nine yards, then eight yards, then ten yards on their defense with three straight running plays. The defense showed serious signs of irritation at as we ran the ball on them with ease. Their star end shouted at me with each snap, and yelled at his own teammates in between plays.

We had crossed the ball into their territory, when a forth

run play was called for Donte. This time when I handed the ball off to Donte, he ran straight up the gut, with our offensive line blowing their line back about five yards from my vantage point. Donte had a hole that a truck could drive through and blew through it with a full head of steam. He slipped between the two linebackers and was able to find space in the secondary. He refused to go down and was soon off to the races. He outran every Lovington defensive player on the field until he reached the end zone, giving us a 7-0 lead.

Our defense soon took the field to face their offense for a second time. Over on our sideline we were completely pumped up for Donte's forty-seven yard run for a touchdown. The core had not stopped screaming and we could even hear our fans across the field shouting as well. The Lovington fans sat on their half of the stands silently.

We had stolen the momentum with one play and were ready to get back onto the field and knock those kids in again. It didn't take long for Lovington to tie the game and quiet our crowd down a bit with a broken play in the secondary, allowing for a sixty-yard reception for a touchdown. We knew that Lovington's offense was a big play kind of offense, and if our defense let them score that easily again it was going to put a lot of pressure on our offense to maintain pace with the scoreboard. With the reception going for the touchdown, Lovington had not only tied up the game but had also regained their intensity.

We took the field soon after the kickoff and huddled to call a play. I think everyone in the stadium knew that we were going to run the ball. We had run it four times straight and our line was playing extremely well off the ball at this point. Why fix something that was not yet broken? The defense did not know how to stop Donte so we would give him another chance for another big gain on the ground.

I called, "Go!" and the ball was snapped into my hands. Then I turned to hand the ball off to Donte but once he touched it he quickly realized there was really nowhere to go after his first few steps forward. The nose tackle had jumped the snap and had gotten through Archie with ease. The nose tackle wrapped Donte up and stood him straight up. Donte, did not go down with ease. He kept his feet moving forward, refusing to go down. When there was no more forward progress to be made, the whistle blew right as their star defensive end had taken part in the tackle. This whistle had clearly blown twice and what happened next went beyond playing after the whistle had blown. The end had lifted Donte clear off of the ground, spun around, with him in his arms, and body slammed straight down on his shoulder.

When he hit the ground, every member of the core and those cheering for Hagerman stood and starting screaming at the referees. The referees all threw their yellow flags in the hit's direction. It was one of the worst after the whistle hits I had ever seen, and Donte made no move to get up. He lay on his shoulder crying out in pain. I had a clear view of it all and was infuriated. When their defense end stood up with a smile on his face, I became enraged. He wasn't going for the tackle but was head-hunting. He had seriously hurt one of my boys. Without thinking about the consequences, I launched myself at the defensive end shoving him off of Donte. I only shoved him once, but I made it count, knocking him back on his ass.

He got up quickly and raced toward me cussing. I pointed

in his direction and shouted, "You piece of shit, motherfucker."

We both had to be restrained by our teams. My boys were all yelling at them and them at us. The only reason they had restrained us and did not partake in the scuffle, was our teams did not want either of us kicked out of the game. Fortunately, the refs did not see what happened between us but the trainers had raced onto the field to check on Donte.

The trainers remained out there for a while before helping Donte from the field. His shoulder hung awkwardly down, and had to be supported.

The offense took the field and the back up running back, Tom Quick, followed us ready to fill in as the running back. The coaching staff knew that we were going to have to abandon the run if Quick did not produce on the ground, which he was not able to. He was unable to find the holes in the defense multiple times, making us a one dimensional football team, only throwing it to gain any yards. The problem was the defense knew that we were going to throw the ball more often than not, and they set their defense to prepare for it. When we did try and catch them off guard and run the ball, they managed to get through and stop Quick in the backfield.

By half time, Lovington had scored ten points to our seven. Our momentum was all but gone as we staggered into the locker room.

The life had been sucked out of our crowd as they looked upon us with discouragement. Lovington, on the other hand, was confident going into half, since they were in a good position to pull this game out. Their defense successfully could read our offense and had made all the necessary adjustments to counteract our plays. At half, we had thrown the ball more than twenty times compared to the six times we had run the ball, after Donte had left the game.

As I sat in the locker room, I tried to figure out what had gone wrong with our offense. Our defense had been playing their asses off, giving up only three points since that big play back in the first quarter.

We, as an offense, had put a lot of pressure on them in the first half yet we were lucky to even be in this game. Thinking about the first half, my stomach was tied in knots. This was not the way I had imagined this game going and I could blame the imbalanced play calling all I wanted, but I knew the bottom line there was no one to blame but myself. As the quarterback, it started and ended with me. For the first time, I took responsibility for my team's performance. Damn it, I was going to do something about it. This was what Coach Castro meant before the game against Dexter. "We'll find out what type of player you are, Rocky, when everything goes to hell."

We had lost our starting running back and our backup was not able to get the job done. Because of this, Coach had strayed from the original game plan of maintaining a balance play calling system, and was putting the game in my hands. He knew we would win or lose the game based on my arm. He must have had faith in me to do this.

I was not going to let him or the rest of this team down. It was time to take this team to a new level. When halftime had eroded, the coaches told us all of the adjustments that needed to be made in the second half. I was ready to change the pace of this game.

As we charged out from the locker room and onto the football field, I caught a glimpse of Karen with her cheerleading team. She smiled at me as if to say to me she knew I could do it.

Brogan and Beal were yelling at Brett and me from the stands in their best attempt to motivate us. The rest of the core remained quiet for the most part. Even though we were only down by three points, it felt as if we were down by twenty-one points.

I stood in a corner of the field by myself waiting for the kick off. I was in my own little zone and planned to do something that I had never done before. I would lead a team from behind, when everything had gone to hell. The old Rocky would have just quit on himself and his team, but not this Rocky. He would take charge of this game.

I took to the field after we'd returned the ball, lining up on our thirty-yard line. The offense huddled and I called out the passing play to my guys, but I had no intention of throwing the ball. After the huddle had broken up, we lined up in our formation and I started to read the defense. They had lined up in their conservative formation, figuring that I was going to pass the ball.

"Go!" I yelled, as the ball was snapped back to me. I dropped back three steps and planted my foot as usual but this time I started to run forward through the holes in the defensive line. I found a hole and managed to slip by the front line. The linebackers recognized what I was doing and charged me from the zone coverage. They met me close to the first down marker where I lowered my right shoulder and unloaded one hell of hit, knocking the linebacker back on his ass.

The moment I hit him, the defense end who had taken out Donte hit me from behind, pushing me over the first down marker. "You motherfucker," he shouted. The end tried talking shit to me, but I did not even bother getting into him, standing up and organizing my team into a hurry up offense.

Coach Castro had told the offense he wanted me to pick the pace with the offense, by doing the hurry up, calling the plays at the line of scrimmage, not allowing Lovington to make any substitutions.

I quickly called the play at the line and snapped the ball moments after. The defense again thought I was going to throw the ball, dropping back into coverage. I saw the linebackers take a few steps back. I cut forward and tucked the ball into my body, running straight at them.

When I met a linebacker head on, I lowered my shoulder and hit him with everything I had. I gained another ten yards before he brought me down, but his head was sure ringing after that hit. Then I stood quickly, and rushed the offense to the line of scrimmage calling a pass play based on how the defense was lined up. This time when I snapped the ball for the third play on the drive, the linebackers were keying on me. They assumed I would run at them again. I threw the ball right over their heads, into Brett's hands who ran up field for a big gain of twenty-two yards and into Lovington's territory.

The crowd suddenly came back to life, yelling with every play. I maintained the same style of play through the drive, taking whatever the defense gave me. When the linebackers dropped back into coverage. I tucked the ball and ran straight at them for a gain of at least five every time. When they keyed on me running the ball and didn't drop back, they made it that much easier for me to find Steven, Brett, and Arturo, who were all running short routes.

We had managed to get the ball to the two-yard line, the

situation being first and goal. Lovington's defense was clearly frustrated the entire drive but were now focused. They knew that this drive was a big one, and if we could put points on the board, it would be a huge confidence boost for the entire team, not to mention every Colts fan would erupt.

We lined up in a power formation, with the intent to run the ball until we got into the end zone. We ran it twice in a row and both times Quick was stopped at the line of scrimmage. The core and our team was now nervous that we weren't going to be able to get into the end zone, after such an incredible second half opening drive.

If we could not get the ball into the end zone, we would have to take the points and kick the field goal, which would be more of a moral victory for Lovington than us. Lining up with it being third and goal, I felt calm and steady. Lovington's defense looked pumped confident they could stop us, unaware what was about to hit them.

I snapped the ball and turned to Quick to hand him the ball, but at the last moment I pulled it back and out of his hands in a designed play action. After faking the hand off and tucking the ball, I rolled out to look for Arturo who was my only throwing option running a drag route behind the defense. He was supposed to be running parallel with me but he had been tripped up coming off of the ball.

The right defense end had keyed on me once I had snapped the ball and sprinted at an angle that would allow him to bring me down if I did not decide what to do with the ball. At the last second as the right end was about to get his hands on me, I tucked the ball into my body and ran for the corner of the end zone.

One of Lovington's linebackers had recognized the action play and ran parallel to me a couple yards behind the end zone line. He knew immediately when I tucked the ball what I was trying to do and he broke for the corner of the end zone. I had managed to turn the corner running out of the grasp of the defensive end. Now it was between the linebacker and me, both of us in a total sprint for that corner. I knew the linebacker was going to get me so I launched my entire body and reached for the end zone.

He too hurled himself at me, trying to knock me out of bounds. I landed on the ground, flying up the side then rolling over after being hit. I had lost possession of the ball but because I had rolled out of bounds, it didn't matter. I turned over to try and look at the referee to see what his signal was if we got into the end zone. Suddenly, I found myself swarmed by my entire offense screaming, "You got in, you got in!"

I had scored the touchdown! Once again putting us in the lead.

That was how things went down for our offense the rest of the game. We were able to move the ball on their defense. There was still a lot of crap going on back and forth between both of our teams, with the referees unable to get control of either team. Lovington's offense, like ours, was moving the ball easily down the field.

Normally, when our offense got on a roll, we would blow out opposing teams. But not tonight. Lovington continued to score every time we scored, forcing us into an offensive shoot out.

Midway through the fourth quarter, we finally got a break. We were up 35-32 and Lovington was driving the ball.

However, right as they crossed the fifty, their quarterback threw an interception to one of our corners.

We had finally created the turnover that we needed to take total control of this game. The momentum built inside me. The Hagerman crowd was the loudest it had been all night, knowing we needed to score to guarantee the win. I stood in front of my offense with total and complete confidence.

"Ready, set, go!" I said dropping back five steps to give Brett enough time. I looked in his direction and he had beat the corner broke to the middle, thirty yards down field. All I needed to do was throw him the ball and he would have an easy touchdown. When he planted his foot into the ground and cut to the center of the field, I planted my back foot, and stepped forward to throw the ball. My knee was straight as I transitioned my weight forward to give the ball the necessary velocity to get to Brett who was open deep down the field.

As I released the ball, my weight was completely forward but what I did not see was that their star defense end had managed to get through Borris. He catapulted himself at me so I would throw the ball off target and his helmet went straight into my front knee, which was almost locked when I threw the ball. His hit disrupted my throw as the ball sailed over Brett's head for an incomplete pass. At that moment, the game slid into slow motion. The pain in my knee was so excruciating I nearly passed out.

A lot of linemen were convinced Lovington's star defensive end had hurt me intentionally. Maybe he did. They shoved him off of me but he got right back up and right in Archie's face. Archie stood toe-to-toe with him. "Who the fuck you think you are?" Archie shouted through his facemask.

"Just doing my job, motherfucker," Lovington's star defensive end yelled back.

Members of both teams pushed and shoved at each other. My right tackle stood over me to make sure no one took a cheap shot at me while I was down. Brett ran over to me to see if I was all right, but I knew something was wrong.

I lay on the ground holding my knee praying that I had not blown it out. The crowed started yelling, like they did when they saw the dirty hit on Donte. It was clear to everyone that the same Lovington player had purposely gunned for my knee.

Moments later, the crowd became silent when I didn't get up. The pushing and shoving continued above me with the referees trying to separate everyone. I felt like it took forever, but the trainers finally managed to get to me. One of them shook his head as he peered down at me. "Where does it hurt?"

All I could do was point to my knee, moaning in pain. While they examined my knee I kept replaying the hit over and over in my mind. When his helmet collided with my knee, it felt like someone had taken a sledgehammer to it. I was terrified to even move it, not knowing what would happen if I did. The trainers lifted me up and helped me off of the field. The crowd shouted my name clapped their hands. Everyone knew if I this was a season ending injury, the Hagerman team would be done.

Even though the trainers were supporting the majority of my weight, I tried to put some weight on my hurt knee and was surprised that I could. When I got to the sideline, Coach Lou called for Kenny Armstrong, my back up, to get into the game. I knew that the sophomore was not ready, but focused on my knee for the time being.

They took me to the training table where the training staff evaluated my injury. While they examined my knee, I tried to see Armstrong out there. I was disappointed to see him quickly back on the sideline, telling me that the offense could not move the ball, forcing us to punt the ball back to Lovington. This gave them the chance to take the lead, and possibly win the game.

Cadets behind me shouted words of encouragement to me hoping that my injury was not that bad. After the offense had come off of the field, Coach Castro walked up to me sitting on the trainer's table.

"How bad is it?" he asked the trainer.

He glanced at the coach then looked down at me. "Not that bad, actually."

"Do you know what he did?"

"From the looks of it, it looks like he just hyper extended his knee."

"What does that mean?" I asked.

"You know when you jam your finger, when playing basketball or something," the trainer said. "Well, it's like that, except for this time you did it with you leg."

"Can I play?"

"I wouldn't recommend it. There really is not much more damage you can do it, but trust me, it will hurt like hell. Chances are you won't even be that effective if you go back out there."

"I understand, but can I play?"

"If it came down to it, yeah you can play."

When I heard this news I looked at Coach Castro, with my eyes wide open.

"Why don't you try and walk around on it," Coach Castro said.

I hopped off of the table and started to walk around the area, with a slight limp. I tried hard to keep a straight face to show that each step I took did not hurt that much, but inside every step felt like a thousand daggers where being jammed straight into my knee cap. Yet I was able to convince Coach Castro that I could go back in.

He put his arm around my shoulders. "Follow me and let's see what Coach Lou says."

As we looked to find Coach Lou, Lovington's offense threw a deep pass into the end zone to their top receiver for a touchdown, taking the lead 39-35. When we reached Coach Lou, he was fuming at what had just happened. With a little more than two minutes left in the game we needed to score nothing less than a touchdown to seal this victory from Lovington.

I smiled at Coach Lou. "Trainer says I'm good, Coach."

Coach Lou cocked an eyebrow. "Really? What did he say it was?"

"I hyperextended my knee. He said it was nothing serious and that I could still play."

"He said that?"

"Well, he did say it would probably hurt like hell but other than that it wouldn't cause any more damage."

"There's no way you can go out there, Rocky. I'm sorry."

"Coach, I can do it. I can win this game for you. We have two minutes and fifteen-seconds to march down the field and punch in a touchdown. We both know Armstrong can't do this against this defense. Maybe one day he will develop into a fine quarterback but he is not ready for this. I can do it, Coach, I am ready."

"And what about your knee? How do you expect to drop back if it hurts like hell? How do you expect to move around if you can only barely walk?"

"Put me in a shot gun formation every play and run quick routes like we did in Dexter. I will get the ball out of my hands in less than two-seconds not allowing the defense a chance to touch me."

Coach Lou scratched his head and didn't say anything for a long moment. As the ball was kicked off to us he looked over at Coach Castro. "What do you think, Castro?"

"He gives us the best chance to win this game," Coach Castro said.

Again, another pause before Coach Lou looked me in the eye. "You get that ball out of your hands in less than two-seconds. If you hold that ball for any longer and they start getting free shots at you, I will take you out of the game so fast that it will make your head spin."

I smiled back at him, put my helmet on. "Understood."

The entire crowed stood and roared as they saw me with my helmet on. I had moments before I was going to take the field and try and win it for and the game. I knew that this drive was going to be the most difficult drive I had ever done in my entire life, because of the injury to my leg. The coaches knew that my leg was hurting but had no idea how excruciating the pain was or that it was worsening with each step I took.

As I took to the field, the crowd shouted "Rocky! Rocky!" My offense cheered me on as I rejoined them in the huddle.

"Okay, boys," I said. "We are going to go into a hurry up

offense. We will be doing only short and quick passes because I won't be able to drop back or move around. Line, give me two-seconds, that's all I need."

"We got you, Rock," Archie said.

I called the play in the huddle and looked into each of their eyes through their helmets. Every one of them looked mesmerized at the fact that I was standing there in the huddle after a hit assuming I had blown out my knee. As they stared into my eyes I felt their trust. They believed I knew what I was doing being out there again, and they were ready to do everything that they could to win this game. I don't know if it was me being out there or if it was the crowd, or the opponent, but in that huddle was a renewed sense of motivation to win the game.

I limped to my position in shot gun formation and shouted out the cadence. I was calm and focused staring into the eyes of the defense telling them with my eyes that they weren't finished with me yet and that I had one more trick up my sleeve.

"Go!" I called and the ball snapped back into my hands. I looked at Brett who had just made his cut, brought my arm back, and flung the ball into his hands for a short gain. It took less than a second for the ball to leave my hands and I knew it was going to have to be that quick for me to remain untouched.

I limped into position. My knee hurt more than ever. I tried to zone the pain out calling out the new play to my offense at the line of scrimmage. Once everyone knew their jobs I quickly snapped the ball, stood for a moment, and threw the ball to Steve who had just run a short hook pattern. He turned after catching the ball for a gain of six yards and a first down.

The ball was on our twenty-nine yard line with a minute

and fifty-seconds to go in the forth. I tried to hurry everyone to the line of scrimmage, knowing that time was not any ally to our team. With every step I took, the limp had become worse and worse. I could no longer hide my pain in my face as there was a grimace with every step I took to get to the line. Coach Lou had run out of time outs to call to try and get me off of the field, and I knew I was the guy, with or without my leg, and everyone on my team and in the stands, cheering for us, was looking at me to suck it up and giving everything I had.

Archie ran up to me, "You all right?"

"Don't worry about me, man. Get to the line right now," I said pointing him to his position.

I finally got to the line where my team was already lined up waiting for me. I knew I was hurting the team with how slow I was getting to the line, but I had to keep going. I couldn't give into the pain.

I barked the play to my players and quickly snapped the ball. I first looked at Brett again but noticed Arturo streaking up the center of the field, blowing by linebackers. I floated the ball just over the reach of those linebackers and into Arturo's hands. He then turned and ran for another ten yards before being brought down by one of their safeties, for a gain of close to twenty yards and into their territory.

With the catch the majority of my offense started to run to the line of scrimmage for the next play. I was left behind trying to hop to the line. The pain was so bad I couldn't even put any weight on my leg. I looked up to see that the clock was about to hit one minute. A part of me began to panic, thinking that I was going to lose this game because I couldn't make it to the line in between plays. The core shouted my name while

Lovington's players were yelling at me to quit. "No way, give up, you idiot," they shouted.

As I hopped to the line, I felt two massive shoulder pads come from underneath me to lift me clear up in the air. Both Archie and Borris had come from behind me and had lifted me clear off the ground and were now carrying me to the ball. They took me straight to my position and went to their own on the line.

I called the play at the line, telling my receivers to run a short quick slant. They did so for a short gain and like the last time Archie and Borris carried me to the line. This kept on happening over and over again. They knew my leg was shot to hell and that they needed to help me in order to save us some time. Our offense repeated throwing short routes and we slowly but surely moved the ball. However, the clock had just dipped below thirty-seconds and we were sitting first and ten with twenty-five yards separating us from victory. Knowing this, I snapped the ball on first and ten and threw it straight into the ground, spiking it, to stop the clock.

With time to kill, Archie called for a huddle, allowing us to form up and run a specific play. "Shot gun, x route, zigzag, cross," I told my offense. "Brett, that corner is going to be playing you tight, thinking that you are running a quick route. I want you to run a stop and go."

"What about the play, Rock?"

"The hell with the play, trust me. When you run the hook route, the corner will bite and commit to defending the short pass. When he does that, you turn straight for that end zone. I'll hit you in stride."

"Man, but your knee," Brett said. "I'll need about five-seconds to get out there, and if you can't move around in the pocket, you will be a sitting duck."

"My line will give me five-seconds," I said looking at all five of my lineman.

"You will have six," Archie said with confidence.

"Good," I said. "Now do it Brett and let's shock these cocky sons of bitches."

We broke from the huddle and went to stand in our positions. I gazed over the defense as if to pretend that I was trying to read them, when in fact, I knew from the moment I lined up in shotgun formation, where I was going to put the ball. They were over there talking shit to me and my offense, but I knew that was just because they were scared that they were going to lose to a gimp.

"Ready," I said with a calmness about me, as if I knew how this game was going to end. "Set," I said with a tone to the defense, letting them know that they have no idea who they were fucking with. "Go!" I yelled, sending a message to the defense that I was about to stun them into tomorrow.

The ball was snapped back into my hands and everything went in slow motion for me. I first looked off to the safeties in Steven's direction, allowing the safeties to think that I was going to him. Through the corner of my eye, I saw Borris cut block Lovington's star defense end. The rest of the line was blocking with an intensity that I had never seen before. The pocket was maintained as I had hoped it would, when an outside linebacker shot through the line unblocked.

With him barreling down on me, I prepared to be hit, unable to move away. Just as he was about tackle me, Quick stepped up and laid a block on the linebacker knocking him to the ground. With Quick's block, I looked up in Brett's direction. The five-second, internal clock, was about to run out in my mind, and I was counting on Brett to make his break for the end zone. As I looked up, Brett was running up the sideline wide open, with his right hand in the air signaling me.

I stepped forward onto my bad leg. The pain sheered up my leg and through my body. With a clear throwing path and no one barreling down on me, I launched the ball high into the air.

The ball soared through the air in Brett's direction. While the ball was in flight, everyone had stopped blocking and hitting and was watching the ball in the air. I glanced at Brett, trying to gauge where he was compared to the ball, and I knew when he began to hold his hands almost to basket catch it, I had thrown in perfectly.

He reached up and brought the ball in for a touchdown giving us the lead with less than fourteen-seconds in the game.

Everyone from Hagerman was cheering as Brett crossed the end zone to score the game-winning touchdown. My line picked me up and carried me to the celebration going on, on the sideline. Players were jumping on each other with total excitement. The core was going insane in the stands as if we had just won the State Championship. Brogan and Beal were shouting my name from the stands. Brett appeared from nowhere and gave me a huge hug. "That was the craziest thing I've ever seen."

"Can't believe you pulled that one off," said Coach smiling as I headed off the field. "You are nuts continuing out there with that knee."

When the game ended fourteen-seconds later on a

desperation hail marry from Lovington that fell way short, every cadet stormed onto the field. It took a while, but our team managed to make our way back into the locker room. We were jumping around and screaming, thrilled that we had just beaten our most hated rival.

Through all of the celebrating, Archie managed to find me and put his arm around my shoulder. "What you just did out there was the bravest thing I've ever seen someone do for this team. I'm proud to call you my quarterback."

No one had ever said something like that to me before in my life. In the past, I'd been thought of as an arrogant player who only cared for himself. Hearing those words from a person I followed and admired in the core was something I took to heart.

Chapter Sixteen

There were sixteen teams that had made the playoffs, eight on opposite sides of the bracket. Researching all of the potential teams that we would possibly have to play, I was confident that we could beat each of them without much of a struggle except St. Michaels of Santa Fe, the number one seed in the opposite bracket. We would not have to face this team unless we both made the State Championship.

St. Michael's quarterback had been signed by Ohio State, which told me he'd be the best quarterback I had ever had to face if our teams met. They had a high power offense like ours by putting up a lot of points with every game they had played.

St. Michaels had beaten a lot of quality opponents. What really stuck out to me wasn't their unblemished record, but one victory they had earned late in the season destroying Eldorado High School of Albuquerque. Eldorado, like Lovington, was in a class above us. The fact that they had blown them out of the game, winning 49-6, made me nervous. At first, I thought it was a mistake. But after looking at Eldorado's schedule, they had in fact been blown out by St. Michael's football program. We beat a similar opponent, in Lovington, but we came out of that game winning by the skin of our teeth. We'd be up against a high-powered offense that our defense would really struggle to slow down. It most likely would end up in a shoot out. I didn't like shootouts because just one turnover mistake can cost your team the game. And this game would be the State Championship.

All week and during practice I studied the statistics of St. Michael's team instead of focusing on our first opponent. I thought they would be an easy win and didn't need much review. The coaching staff noticed that I wasn't in the film room as much as I had been in the past to prepare for the eight-seeded Estancia. For the most part they let me do my thing, because I had shown them all season that no matter what, I showed up to the game fully prepared.

I don't know why I didn't take time to prepare for Estancia. I lay in bed at night wondering where my motivation had gone. It had nothing to do with my relationship with Karen, nor was it the core. I had managed to handle everything going on with that stress, making every formation and staying out of trouble. I had a couple of demerits and only one tour to march over the weekend but that was not that big of a deal.

Brett and my other friends all tried to get me out of my funk but I had little interest in hanging out with anyone and stayed pretty much to myself. I did still get together with Karen, but even after long discussions at night with her I couldn't escape from the depression I was feeling. It was like I was mentally and physically exhausted from everything that had gone on. I felt like a zombie going from class to class and then to practice every day without a break. It affected my performance come game time in the first round of the playoffs. We barely won by one point in an ugly game against Estancia, a team I thought would be an easy win. I ended up throwing two interceptions with no touchdowns. The touchdowns we did get came from the defense in a pick six, and the special teams who had returned a kickoff back for a touchdown. Ultimately, it was the defense who won the game for us keeping Estancia's offense out of the end zone for the most part.

The next day watching film, all of the coaches were furious with the offense and especially me. "You were playing like a bunch of mindless idiots who had never stepped onto a football field," said Coach Castro eyeballing me the whole time he spoke. Then he pulled me aside after practice. "If you don't get your shit together, Montoya, this team won't survive another playoff game and we'll be out in the second round."

Even that did not create the motivation I needed to win games and to lead the team. I stormed back to my room around noon on a Saturday and lay in my bed. I prayed it was the lack of sleep that had created this funk. I desperately wanted to find the motivation once more for this last run. Everyone was counting on me and I was letting them down. Just like I had let people down back in Texas. It was happening again before my eyes, and I felt powerless to do anything to change this inevitable outcome.

As I dozed off, there was a knock on the door. When I opened the door, Karen stood in the doorway out of uniform and in a pair of jeans and a T-shirt. She held a bag over her shoulder and glared at me with a smile. "Got any crazy plans for the rest of the weekend?"

"You know, I was thinking about playing military for the weekend. The usual stuff." I said sarcastically.

She laughed. "Change into some normal clothes and meet me in the parking lot after you sign out with one of the Company Officers."

"You're kidding me right?"

She smiled. "Today's the first weekend RATs are given permission to take their first mini furlough."

"Oh, crap, I totally forgot about that."

She took my hand. "So, unless you have something better to do, let's get out of here for the rest of the day and tomorrow."

"Where do you want to go? It's not like there is a whole lot around here."

"Why do you always think I don't have a plan? Just get dressed and meet me by the car. Trust me, what I have planned is a hell of a lot better than sticking around here."

After she left, I pulled out some clothes I'd brought from my old life in Texas. It was such a strange feeling sliding into a pair of jeans. I threw a bag together with a change of clothes with the assumption that I wouldn't be back for the night and made my way to my Company Officer's office to take my first furlough.

Signing out with Captain O'Malley was a quick process. I needed to be back by five o'clock the next afternoon. I sprinted to the parking lot where Karen waited for me in the car. It would be the first time I could sleep somewhere other than my shitty bunk. No bugles, no yelling, and no stress from anything. I felt like I was going on an extravagant vacation.

Karen gave me a passionate kiss when I reached her car. This vacation had already started with a bang. She took the wheel and I sat shotgun as we drove south to Second Street and turned on the highway straight out of town. We opened the windows and let the music blare out. It had been such a long time since I had been somewhere other than Roswell.

The scenery included mountains surrounding the entire area, with plateaus off in the distance. The weather cooperated at 70 degrees, contributing to making this a most memorable day.

I had no idea where we were going, but I really did not care. The only thing that mattered was the road ahead. I felt an overwhelming sense of freedom, and I didn't want the drive to end. I took Karen's hand in mine, and felt like life couldn't get better than this.

We drove for about an hour before reaching Ruidoso, where we had played our first game of the season. I never really got to see the town because of that game, but driving in with Karen I now had the opportunity to appreciate the quaint town that was embedded in the mountains. Every building appeared as if it had been recently constructed. The people meandering from building to building wore fashionable clothing and smiled as they chattered with each other. After going to a lot of small-depressed towns in New Mexico, this one appeared prosperous and was by far the nicest one I'd been to in all of the state.

Karen stopped the car and smiled at me. "Want to spend the night here?"

"I couldn't think of a better place," I said. "Is this your first time in Ruidoso?"

"I've been here a few times. I like to come up here especially on furloughs. It's one of my favorite towns in the area."

"I am starting to think the very same thing."

We kept on driving through the town for a while before Karen pulled up into the parking lot of a hotel. "How are we going to pay for this?" I said, embarrassed that I didn't have the money.

"Don't worry. The owner's a Hagerman graduate and I know him pretty well," she said.

I followed her into the lobby carrying the bags from the car. We made it through the check-in process quickly. We ambled to the elevator and got off on the fifth floor. When I opened the door, it felt like I had opened the door into heaven. The room had one queen-sized bed with an incredible view of the mountains from the balcony. The room felt like a breath of fresh air, it was so clean. I couldn't remember having ever slept in such an upscale room. The white sheets were clean and crisp. Try as we may, Brett and I had nothing on the hotel's cleaning service. It was the nicest room I'd ever slept in.

Once settled, we didn't leave the room until night had fallen on the city of Ruidoso. We held each other's hands and walked a few blocks to an Italian restaurant where we ate some of the best Chicago-style pizza. The perfect meal for the perfect day. Then we went to see that new romantic movie, Love and Other Drugs.

The only cloud that night was that we both knew our time together was very limited. There was hardly a minute where one of us was not touching the other, holding hands, kissing, or me having my arm around her. It was the most magical time I had ever spent with another person. We laughed at silly jokes we only got, and talked about our dreams and goals for the future.

After making love another time late that night, I couldn't sleep. Karen fell off really quickly. She looked line an angel with her long hair splayed all over the pillow. I lay in the bed next to her, tossing and turning for hours. The sleeplessness was a result of the same thing that had created my funk for the past week since I'd looked at St. Michael's stats online. Yet I was just too afraid to admit to myself what was going on.

Finally, around three in the morning, I got out of bed and walked to the balcony where I stood staring at the mountain range. I thought that maybe something as beautiful as a mountain range would calm me down and relax me, but it didn't help.

As I turned to return to the bed, Karen stood behind me. "What's wrong, baby?"

"Nothing. I didn't mean to wake you up. Lets go back to bed."

She blocked my path back to the bed. "Is there something on your mind?"

"It's nothing that I can't handle."

She narrowed her eyes. "You know, I have known all week that something was upsetting you."

"I don't want to bother you with my problem."

"I'm your girlfriend. It's my job to be here when you need me and you need me now."

She was right. I did need someone at that moment and she was the closest person to me. I trusted her completely. After coming to this understanding, I broke the silence. "I'm afraid."

"Afraid of what?"

I looked down, took a deep breath, thinking I had never been so vulnerable to another person in my entire life. "Failure."

We both sat down on the edge of the bed. "What do you mean?"

"I am supposed to fail around this time."

"I don't understand, Rock."

"My whole life, before this year I have always let everyone down. I don't even have a family because of it. My father wanted no part of me. That was obvious when he left a long time ago. My mother recently decided she too wanted nothing to do with me. Jesus, I don't even know when the last time I talked to her. I let her down as a son and she's given up on me."

"Baby, I am so sorry," she said with tears forming in her eyes. "Did you ever think that maybe there was something wrong with your parents? That is wasn't anything you did? What kind of father abandons his son? What kind of mother doesn't support her child through the bad times?"

"It's not even that. I have accepted that my family doesn't want anything to do with me, and I am okay with that, because I have made myself a new family. Those guys on the football team are my brothers. They are my only family that I have."

Karen took my hand in hers. "That's wonderful."

"The thing is," I said. "I am afraid to let them down, like I have let everyone else down in the past."

"You won't let them down."

"How do you know that? That's all I do. When things are going good I find a way to mess up. It's almost as if when things are going well I start to think that they are too good to be true and that something is going to happen to bring my world crumbling to the ground. I am afraid that they will all be looking for me to lead them to victory and the championship. There is that little demon inside me whispering to me, telling me that I am going to fail. Any minute I am going to fail and let everyone down."

After spilling my guts, Karen squeezed my hand tighter.

It was strange that I felt no sadness. I was beyond the point of feeling sorry for myself. I did feel bad for those I had to lead.

As if Karen read my mind she said, "The moment you say you can't is the moment you lose."

"What do you mean?"

"It's something I read somewhere. When you say you can't do something in your mind, your body believes that you are going to fail and more often than not you will fail. Listen to me, and listen good. I didn't know you before you put the uniform on and called yourself a Hagerman cadet. I don't know the type of person you used to be and frankly it really doesn't matter. I know you as the man you are today and I will tell you, you are one hell of a person. What you have done with this team is incredible. You are in a situation unique to all others. Most people get to concentrate on school, their social life, and football, but not you. You have so many more responsibilities essentially forcing you to become an adult earlier than most. The fact that you are able to do all of the things you do every day and still manage to be successful on the field is something that truly is amazing. I know a lot of people who could not do what you do. Most don't even try because it is simply too goddamn hard. But you're special, Rocky. You really are. I look at you and I don't see the arrogant kid you've described yourself to be. I see someone with an incredible passion for not only himself, but the people around him."

She went on, "You have to let go of the past. You have to or it will destroy you. If you only got to see what all of us see every single day when we look into your eyes you would be amazed at the person you are. You're not a follower on the field. You're not even a great player out there, you go beyond that. You're a game changer. People like you are so rare and they hardly even have the ability to recognize how great they truly are. But I see that greatness in you and you need to see it too. When you finally do realize how incredible you are, Rock, there's nothing that will stand in your way. Don't let your past destroy you. Let it fuel you to become a better all around you."

I felt like a massive weight had been lifted off of my shoulders. Karen was right. Everything she said was right. The only thing holding me back was me. I needed to let go and stop fighting myself. In that moment, not only did I realize what Karen had seen in me, but I forgave everyone who had let me down. And then, most importantly of all, I forgave myself. It was the most powerful thing I had ever experienced and finally I felt like I could move forward. Finally, I felt motivated to finish this season with everything I had in me. I was ready to finish what I had started here at Hagerman and become someone I had always wanted to become.

We spoke little to each other on the drive home but instead just listened to the music from the radio as the wind passed through our hair from the open windows. We held hands and I felt closer to her than I'd ever been with anyone in the world. I was incredibly grateful for all of Karen's insight. Her words let me finally let go of my fear for failure and had reestablished the fire in the pit of stomach to get back to work on the football field.

No longer did I obsess with St. Michael's statistics or their successes throughout the season. I was now focused on what I needed to do in order to get ready to play Los Alamos High this upcoming Friday. We had dodged a bullet with Estancia, mainly because of me, and I knew that, and I was not going to let that happen again under my watch. The players had worked their asses off to get to this position and now they looked at me to lead them. If I couldn't do my job, it would be the reason why this season was going to be cut short. I would no longer take any opponent for granted. Every team we faced would have my utmost attention and they would regret the day they thought they had a chance at keeping pace with us. I made a promise to myself on that drive back to Hagerman that I would come back with a vengeance, come back stronger, smarter, and better than anyone who dared to face me. I would make sure I was the best damn player on that field, and those standing opposite me were going to know it.

CHAPTER SEVENTEEN

It was almost a relief to get back into the film room and back to work. Not only was it a relief for me but also for my fellow teammates and coaches. They knew that I was not acting like I normally did, but when they saw me get back to work, they became more relaxed. The coaches all knew that I took a mini furlough and figured that all I needed to do was to get away for a while. Now that I was back, it was all business and no play. I got through my daily core activities as quickly and as efficiently as possible. I attended my classes and studied and spent every last free moment going over film with anyone who was willing to put in the extra effort as well.

I had also returned to my old self at practice. With each snap I ran the play as if it were a game situation. The weather had become very cold but I wouldn't let that effect my practice performance setting the tone for the whole team. And that was how it went down every weekday after school, moving from week to week, defeating every team that we were assigned to play.

We made our way through the bracket with ease after the Estancia game, and I had regained my focus. No team scored more than 14 points on our defense, and my offense didn't put up anything less than 30 points on the scoreboard. It was obvious to all those around us and especially in the core that this football team was on a mission. With every victory, excitement grew throughout Hagerman including both the cadets and staff. I had regained my celebrity status once again. Wherever I went, everyone throughout the school recognized me and threw words of confidence in my direction. I felt great receiving compliments from officers throughout the core. It really made my day when the Command Sergeant Major stopped me. "You know, Rocky, I've attended Hagerman for six years and this is the first time I've ever really gotten excited over what a sports team here could potentially do. Good luck. Feel assure that the entire core is behind you."

Excitement grew with every victory as we moved closer to the State Championship in Albuquerque. The Commandant decided that he would allow for cadets in good status to travel with the team to Albuquerque, if we were to make it that far. So far, every cadet got to see us play in the playoffs because we were the first seed, which meant that every team we faced had to come to Roswell to play us. Even though it was sometimes freezing, the crowds filled the stands at every night game cheering us on.

Beal and Brogan were our biggest fans. Beal always waited for Brett and me after the game near the locker room to congratulate us on our performance. She was such a sweet friend and I appreciated her support. Karen, of course was always there and we'd often sneak off after the games. She never said, "I told you so," but I knew if it hadn't been for her helping me regain my confidence, none of this would ever have happened. She had this look on her face that made me feel how proud she was of me. I'm not going to lie, that look was damn sexy. I could always see her from the sideline jumping around and screaming with every play. She never failed to bite her nails in stressful situations so although she said she was calm, I knew there were times when she was as nervous as me.

We had finally made it to the week of the State Championship, after nearly a month of playoff football. Like everyone had anticipated, we would face St. Michaels at the end to determine the new State Champion. St. Michaels, like us, had destroyed every opponent they had faced, and looked like they were on a total roll. Their defense was clearly the weakest part of their team, but the offense more than made up for it. Brett and I discussed it. "The defense may be able to slow St. Michael's offense down," he said after practice one night. "But stopping them was going to be damn near impossible."

I was focused all week in practice. If Ruidoso had not happened, with Karen, I would be a wreck leading into this game. I would have dwelled on what had happened in last year's State Championship in Premium when I blew it. But I was not going to worry about things that were in the past that week. I kept telling myself over and over, "You are different, you're not the same, you are changed, and you are going to win this time."

I maintained the positive attitude Karen told me I needed to have and it really did work. Practices were efficient and the players and I were on cue with every play run.

With each practice there would be several news stations surrounding Stapp field, filming our practice, looking for interviews, and watching us get ready for the big game. A lot of the core after their afternoon workout, would come out to Stapp field and watch us practice. They were almost as invested in our campaign as we were and no one was as excited as them. All week we kept on hearing from everyone that nobody knew when the last time Hagerman won a State Championship in football. It was a big deal for them and it was an even bigger deal for us.

The week had finally ended and we were as ready as we were ever going to be. The announcement came at lunch in the mess hall, from the RC that all cadets, in good standing would be permitted to go to Albuquerque for Friday night's game. The buses would load for the core at 3:30 and arrive into University Stadium, at the University of New Mexico by 7:30's scheduled kickoff. The entire core let out a scream when they heard this news and began to cheer in unison, "Let's go, Colts."

Sitting there and listening to it, I thought back on my days back at Premium and I not once remembered the amount of excitement that followed our team throughout the playoffs. That was the reason why I felt that tonight's game was going to be the biggest game of my life. More than a thousand cadets were totally behind us, and I was not just playing for my football legacy and finally getting that ring, but I was playing for them. We all were forced to live on a daily basis with stress and difficulties that no other teenagers had to live with. We were the stars that would show brilliantly through the darkness. This wasn't for me, hell it wasn't even for our team, it was for the core of cadets. We were playing for them.

After lunch, the football team had been put on status, which allowed us to miss class without being stuck. We were supposed to meet in the locker room to get our football gear and head to Honor Street, where the buses waited.

The football team had been granted permission to eat lunch with each other for the day. When the announcement had concluded, we stood and walked to the doors to head for the locker room. The entire core stood and cheered us as we walked through the mess hall. People stuck out their hands to "high five" us. It was probably the coolest thing I had ever done and I could tell a lot of the guys behind me thought the same thing, walking through the mess hall. The recognition continued as we walked through the campus and to the locker room. Those staff members included teachers, company officers, and Commandant staff shouting at us from where they stood to bring home state.

It took awhile, but we finally made it to the buses that we would be taking to Albuquerque, some three hours northwest of Roswell. I sat in my usual seat, closer to the front of the bus and put my headphones on. I stared out the window for the duration of the drive. All that could be seen hour and after hour, was nothing but sand. Off in the distance, were several mountains. It didn't really matter to me. I had entered into my zone and was thinking about the game ahead. I needed to forget how big the game was and perceive it as just another football game.

My attention shifted from the game that I was about to play in several hours. I was no longer thinking about X's and O's nor was I thinking about defensive scheme our game plan. What ran through my mind were flashbacks of what had just happened throughout the past year. I just kept picturing the faces of all of those who had affected me one way or another. I remembered how much I hated Hagerman when I first stood on campus back in August. And now here I was about to give everything I had for those who I used to despise. This was supposed to be a punishment handed down from the courts to me but in reality it was more of a Godsend. The kids on this bus, those in the core, the close friends I had made throughout my time had truly affected change in my life. I no longer was the same person I was this time one year ago. I no longer thought of just myself but cared more for those who have entrusted their faith in me. I was playing for them. I don't know why or even how it happened, but the core was no longer my enemy. It had become my family.

The drive seemed very short as we began to pull into the outskirts of Albuquerque. Looking outside, I realized that this was where Karen was from. It was a fairly large city in my eyes, a boy from a small town in Texas. The city stretched for miles on end. There were majestic mountains to the east of us, the tip of the Rocky Mountain range. To the west were pastel colored mesas.

We drove further into the city and found ourselves in rush hour traffic. To the right of us was Albuquerque's downtown. It was the largest downtown I had ever seen, with large buildings clustered all together.

Finally, the bus pulled up into University Stadium, near the campus of the University of New Mexico. Coach said, "Grab your bags and make your way to the locker room to get settled."

When the team had put all of their pads away and settled in, the coaches came into the locker room. "You guys need to take a walk to get a feel for the field," one of them said.

Exiting the locker room and entering onto the stadium's field, I was thoroughly impressed. The stadium had been built to seat 45,000 people, so it was definitely the largest stadium I had ever walked through. The bleachers surrounded the entire field extending up and outwards. Everything was colored with bright red for the team's colors. What really grabbed my attention, was the tall boxes for fans to sit in. I had never played in a stadium that had box seating, and all I could hope was that they would allow for people to sit in them. For someone like me, I thought that would be awesome.

As we all lumbered around and talked about how cool the stadium was, St. Michael's blue buses pulled up to the stadium. As they exited the buses one of our coaches shouted, "Hagerman team, head to the locker room, to give St. Michaels a chance to walk the field."

We all headed back to the lockers but not without staring back at them all to see what we were up against. From what I could see, those boys were big, telling me that this was going to be a good challenge for us. Not everyone had the same optimism as I had, and those were showing signs of nervousness.

We sat in the locker room with nothing but the game on our mind. The coaches came in and reminded us about the game plan and any last minute changes that they had made. There was really nothing left for us all to do. The guys all tried to act calm and confident, but I could tell that they were all trying to hide how nervous they were. Other than me, not one of the guys had ever played in a State Championship. St. Michaels, on the other hand, was very familiar with this pressure since they were the reigning two time New Mexico State Champions. That experience was something that gave them the advantage on us.

What I have learned, was the team that was the most calm

and collected was the one that played the best. If we went into the game nervous, we would overthink our responsibilities. Once we start thinking in a game that was based more on instinct and reaction, we were all but screwed. Thinking is the killer in football, because when you start to do that, the game moves faster than you are reacting, and that is when you make mistakes, which can lead to a loss. It was most important not to be thinking but to focus our energy to just know each of our jobs, and what needed to be done. Sitting there and looking at my guys, I worried that they were thinking way too much.

With an hour to go before kickoff, Archie came over from his locker and sat next to me, looking straight ahead instead of at me. After a moment, he took a deep breath still looking forward. "What's it like?"

"What's, what, like?" I asked.

Archie raised his eyebrows. "What is playing in a championship like?"

"At first, it's fast. Everyone is flying a million miles an hour, trying to break the ice and take control first. But after each team's first drive, everything slows down for the most part."

"Really? Everything slows down? I would think that it would be fast the whole game."

"No, no," I said with a smile. "You see, after both teams offenses and defenses have been on the field once, and each try and make that big play or that big hit to take command, they then realize that is not how they got there. They will then slow down again, trying to be methodical and try to beat their opponent like they have beaten everyone else."

"So we just can't give them the game in the first drive and then it becomes a chest game."

"Exactly. Everyone just needs to be calm and know what their assignments are," I said. "We can't over think what we need to do. If we start over thinking everything, we are screwed, Archie."

"I know. Trust us, like we trust you, Rock. You make the call and we will all follow you to the end."

I smiled and looked at Archie. "You know, I think that is the first time you have ever called me Rock."

"Yeah, well, don't get used to it," he said grinning. "When I first met you at matriculation, I thought I was going to hate your ass."

"Oh, gee, thanks," I said.

"No, it's true. I thought you were some arrogant punk. But man, I was wrong about you. I have seen such massive strides in you as a leader. What you did with Beal in the confidence course, what you have done with this football team, it's all amazing in my mind. You should know we all our proud to have you as our quarterback, and our leader."

"Thanks a lot, Archie," I said totally humbled. "That means a lot coming from you."

"Yeah, well, again don't get used to it. Win this game tonight and maybe I will let you miss formation from time to time without getting stuck."

"Well, aren't you the best First Sergeant ever," I said laughing and again with a bit of sarcasm.

"Shut up." He stood and walked back to the locker.

The hands slowly moved on the clock and I could not help but to watch it, forcing it to move even slower. With thirty minutes to kick off, the core was just arriving to University Stadium and was probably beginning to fill the stands. I could see Brogan and Beal in the middle of Hotel Company. Brogan probably was getting in trouble one way or another, and Beal was probably in his ear telling him to stop whatever he was doing. I could see them in my mind. And it brought a smile to my face.

I walked around from locker to locker, player to player, talking to each one of them briefly. Not about the game, but about something else. I would talk about stupid sticks people may have gotten stuck for throughout the past week to some guys, and others I would talk to about the Cowboy's season and how hopefully they were going to get that last wild card spot to get into the playoffs. There were a few conversations about girls and some about what some guys had planned on doing after they graduated from Hagerman.

My intention was not to distract the guys about what job they had to do, but to calm them down a bit. I knew that every one of my guys' hearts was racing uncontrollably. Their hands were probably completely wet from all of the sweat, thinking about the time until kick off. That was what it was like for me before the State Championship last year, and I realized that if one of the older guys had come in and tried to calm me down a little, by just talking to me about whatever, the outcome to that game may have been different. I didn't want these guys to ever have to go through what I went through, and I was going to do everything possible to stop that from happening.

Ten minutes before the game Coach Lou entered the room with the entire coaching staff. They sauntered to the front of the locker room where we all could see them. Coach Lou stood in front of all of his staff for a moment in silence while we all stood there waiting for him to say something. What came next, was something none of us anticipated.

"Our deepest fear is not that we are inadequate," he said. "Our deepest fear is that we are powerful beyond measure. It is our light, not our darkness that most frightens us. We ask ourselves, who am I to be brilliant, gorgeous, talented, fabulous? Actually, who are you not to be? You are a child of God. You're playing small does not serve the world. There is nothing enlightened about shrinking so that other people won't feel insecure around you. We are all meant to shine, as children do. We were born to make manifest the glory of God that is within us. It's not just in some of us; it's in everyone. And as we let our own light shine, we unconsciously give other people permission to do the same. As we are liberated from our own fear, our presence automatically liberates others."

We all looked at him in complete and total awe. There was total silence in that locker room as Coach Lou again paused looking downward, then up again at us.

"That was written by Marianna Williamson a while back and it is something that defines this team. I have coached football, now, for more than thirty years, and never have I been a part of a team like this. You, men, are inspiring. There is so much talent and skill on this team, but that's not enough for you. Every day you come to practice and work your asses off, pushing each other, trying to get better. You hang together, when things go bad, and you push and you find a way to win, no matter the cost. Gentleman, I believe we have yet to see the best this team has to offer, and tonight is when we all get the privilege to watch the potential become reality."

With that closing remark he walked through the locker room, with his staff behind him.

Coach Castro, who was right behind Coach Lou gave me a wink. The rest of the locker room remained quiet once they had left. No one had ever seen Coach Lou give some kind of a pep talk in their high school football career not even Archie from the expression on his face. He was the most shocked of all of us. But something he said, about how we have yet to give our best, we have yet to show what this team had to offer, really hit home for all of us.

Our deepest fear is that we are powerful beyond measure. Something from Coach Lou's quote resonated in my mind. I felt like he was talking to me directly and I kept repeating it over and over again before I believed that night, I would become "powerful beyond measure."

I stood and trotted up to my usual spot in front of the team and they formed up in a team huddle around me. There were no words that needed to be said to each other, all that needed to be said was said in the way that we looked at each other there in that moment. We knew all we had for the next two and a half hours was each other. This team was more than a football team, we all were more than friends, we were brothers, and I think in that moment we all recognized what we were to each other. No words, just the moment.

I put my hand up in a fist, for the last time as a Colt's football player and said, "Gentleman, this our time, now let me hear you. One, two, three…"

Everyone, in unison yelled, "OUR TME!" as we broke from the team huddle, and made our way through the locker room doors and onto the field.

CHAPTER EIGHTEEN

Running down the field after breaking through the wall of paper held by Karen and her fellow cheerleaders, I felt the cold air hit my skin through the facemask. The entire football stadium was filled to complete capacity. Half of the fans were dressed in red, to represent our team, while the other half was suited up in blue for St. Michaels. And then there was the core of cadets seated directly behind our bench in their traditional BDUs. As we raced down the field, you could hear the fans cheering for us, but none of them were as loud as the core, who went absolutely ballistic.

It was a great night for football and you could feel the anxiety in the air. The nervous feeling had all of us running completely on adrenaline. As we made it to our sideline, St. Michaels busted through their wall of paper held by their cheerleaders and just like the Hagerman fans the St. Michaels fans too went crazy as their team took the field. Even from where we stood, those boys looked big. Unlike our other opponents who ran their mouths at every opportunity and thought themselves better than everyone, St Michaels was a disciplined team, coached by Pete Rimsha. Rimsha had won five State Championships in twenty years, including the back-to-back championships he had just won for St. Michaels.

We came out strong from the onset and showed that we belonged on the field with these guys. They had rattled us with their experience in big games, but we didn't let them get into our head.

We were a more physical team, while they were more finesse. We couldn't allow ourselves to play their type of game. If we fell into that trap, it would be all but over for us and we would be on that long bus ride home back to Roswell with nothing to show for this incredible season.

I glanced over at St. Michaels, while they took the field from their locker room, and refused to allow myself to be intimidated. Then I turned away and walked up the sideline checking out where Beal and Brogan sat in the stands. Those two were as excited as ever for us and had more confidence than the entire team put together. Beal was yelling in our direction while Brogan was busy screaming at St. Michael's players. "We're gonna kill you guys!" he shouted.

Brett walked up to me. "You ready?"

"I better be," I said with a clumsy smile.

"It's your time to shine as quarterback. What you got yourself here is pretty rare."

I cocked an eyebrow. "And what is that I have, Brett?"

"A second chance. Not many people get a chance to redeem themselves, and you have been blessed with one."

I thought for a second over what he had just said and realized he was right. A second chance to make up for all of the bad I had done in the past to everyone who surrounded me. How many people get a second chance at anything? And competing in the State Championship was an especially rare event.

Brett smiled. "So let's try and not fuck it up this time."

"Don't worry. This time will be different."

His small joke helped to loosen me up, but when the coaches called for the captains to head out to the coin toss, it was all business from that point on.

I stormed onto the field with the other captains, as serious as I had ever been. The moment I touched the field my heart went from racing to calm. My fear dissipated. I was walking to the opposition's captains with confidence. Today they must go through me. That confidence translated over to the other captains who rallied in step with me, chests out and heads held high.

Standing in front of St. Michael's captains, I felt their confidence. Their quarterback, who stood right in front of me, was bigger than me. I had never seen a quarterback stand taller than me before. He had a reputation as a super star, but we'd see if he could live up the hype. As the visitors, we called tails and won the coin toss and elected to kick the ball and give our defense a chance to take the field first. We shook hands with their captains and returned to our sidelines, letting the coaches and all of our players know that we would be kicking to start the game off.

Moments later, the kicking team took the field and kicked the ball off to St. Michaels team to start the game. From that point on, every person in the stadium stood on their feet. I could hear mixed cheers for St. Michaels, from their fans, while at the same time the core was trying to drown them out with cheers in favor of us.

The first few plays, the defense looked strong, establishing themselves on the front line. However, as the drive progressed, their offense started to find holes in our secondary, moving the ball with ease. It didn't take much more than five plays and two first downs for St. Michael's offense to cross over the fifty-yard line into our territory.

Pacing up and down the sideline, watching our defense struggle out of the gate made me nervous. I kept saying underneath my breath, "Come on, stop these guys, stop them."

But we failed to stop St. Michaels as they kept on pushing our defense back and back until they were in the end zone. When they did enter the end zone I buckled my chin strap up and got ready to take the field, knowing it wouldn't be long before I had the chance to respond to the opposition's first drive.

The cheers roared throughout the stadium from St. Michael's fans who jumped up and down in the stands.

My hands began to sweat as pressure on the offense became a reality and I knew we must respond. As an offense we couldn't give them an opportunity to make it a two-possession game. We were now desperate to move the ball. Absolutely, under no condition, could we go three and out. That would demoralize us as a team.

Moments later, the ball was kicked off to our offense to the back of the end zone, giving us a touchback, and placing the ball on our twenty. We were forced to go eighty yards down field to try and tie this game up. I flew onto the field with confidence, with my offense right behind me.

Archie yelled, "Huddle."

That was all I could hear. My prediction had come true,

and the deafening noise that I heard on the sidelines had been drowned out by my concentration. I knew everyone was still yelling, but I no longer heard them.

Donte stood next to me, back from his major injury against Lovington, in the shotgun formation. I called out the cadence, snapping the ball, and handing it off to Donte for a decent gain. It looked from the first play alone, that our offensive line could handle their defensive line. They were big, but my boys had great technique, and were able to get low on them, causing the defensive line to drive back, giving Donte some room to work with.

The play called in the huddle was a play action pass, forcing us to line up in a power I formation. I hated this formation because it did not really give me a great view to read the defense. Still, I called the cadence and snapped the ball, under center. I then turned to Donte, and faked the hand off to him, as he ran up the gut. From there, I ran and curled out of the pocket into open space in the back field and simultaneously looked down field at my receivers to see if anyone was open. I recognized that the defensive end had taken the bait and dove down to try and tackle Donte, allowing me for a wide-open view of the field. There was not a linebacker within fifteen yards of me so I tucked the ball into my body and began to run up field.

This disciplined team had made their first mistake of the game early and I took advantage. I ran up the sideline, where Brett was driving his corner backwards. Trying to gain a few extra yards and cut in, making my way to the middle of the field, crossing our forty yard line. Right when I had made the cut, the linebacker barreled down on me launched himself to try and hit me out of bounds, not thinking that I would cut back in. The cut allowed for him to try and arm tackle me, which was not going to be enough to bring me down. I lifted my shoulder shoving him off me as he hit the ground. His missed tackle opened the field up even further, because of the fact that he was the only linebacker, in the area, who had a chance of bringing me down.

I continued to run down field, as the two safeties tried to catch me to salvage the damage. The strong safety was the first to reach me near the middle of the field. A small guy with a ferocious grin on his face, he left his feet and dove at mine, trying to trip me up. I managed to get the palm of my hand up onto the top of his helmet, allowing for me to push off of it, which stopped him from ever reaching my knees. In doing so, I got spun around for a moment and I almost forgot the direction I needed to run in. I immediately regained my senses and realized that the free safety, the last of the defenses players was right on top of me.

In that instant, I don't know what came over me. I had such an incredible rush of willpower not to go down. In retrospect, I should have been an easy tackle for this guy, because not only did have the angle on me, I had little momentum moving forward. But even though I had seen him out of the corner of my eye, and even though I only had a reaction to get ready for this hit, my will power took over.

As he extended his arms out preparing to wrap me up and bring me to the ground, I lowered my shoulder right in the center of his chest, and threw everything I had into that hit. I smacked him so hard that the guy literally bounced off of me as his helmet went flying off his head ten yards from where he landed.

The hit on this kid opened up the entire field and I took off running. There was no one even close to catching me from behind, as I crossed the forty, than the twenty, than the ten, and finally crossed the goal line for a seventy-five yard run, our team's first touchdown.

I tossed the ball to the ref who had been running stride for stride with me the whole way and turned back to my entire offense, who had raced down field to celebrate the touchdown. They all damn near dog-tackled me, jumping on top of me.

Even though I acted cool in front of the guys, that was the best play I had ever run in my entire life. Both teams had come out onto the field from the start really fired up. Emotions were what would drive the first two series. I felt fortunate to make a big play for my team and tie the game up. Both teams knew that our success had been driven, primarily throughout offense. The defensive teams were good, but they were really nothing compared to the two offenses. After we got off of the field, we calmed down and our nerves were settled. The whole aura of the State Championship had dissipated a bit, and we now acted like it was just a regular football game, like we'd played a hundred different times before.

Back and forth our offenses went, scoring almost at will against the opposition's defense. Every time our offense found a way to punch it into the end zone and tie the game up, St Michaels would take the field and would move to put points on the board and take the lead. For me, it was very frustrating having that much pressure every time I took the field, but I could not allow for my emotions to get the best of me. I couldn't get pissed at the defense for not stopping them. All I could do was my job and wait for our opportunity to take command of this game, because thus far we had been playing catch up.

What we did have to our advantage was time of possession of the ball. Because St. Michaels ran a west coast style of offense in that they threw the ball, nearly eighty percent of the time, they would move the ball on us a lot quicker. Our offense consisted of more of a pro style offense, which really balanced our play call between running and throwing. What gave us the advantage was the fact that because we ran more plays on their defense they grew tired of constantly being on the field. Sooner or later, they would break, and I reassured my offense of this. We needed to stay patient and realized that this game was not a sprint. It was not going to be won a hundred yards at a time, it was going to be one inch by inch, play by play.

"Don't get caught in their style," I told my guys on the sideline. "Play your game, your game is what got us here. Don't play their game."

The intensity rose with every series. Even though the scoreboard indicated that it was a neck-and-neck game, we all felt that St. Michaels was in control. Everyone one of us hoped and prayed that the defense or even the special teams could make a big play and maybe get a turnover to give us the advantage and allow for the offense to have an opportunity to turn the tide. But it did not happen.

The whistle blew at half time. St. Michaels had taken the lead, 35-28 going into half time. It was such a high score for a half and we all knew that. Our offense was worried that the defense was not going to be able to stop them and the defense at the same time was hanging their heads down, knowing it was the offense that was keeping us in the game. I was trying to remain positive in the locker room, talking to only the defensive players, telling them over and over that all it takes is one big play, one big play and the entire first half would be erased. As I spoke, the guys' faces turned from sorrow into that of anger. The coaches came into the locker room and gave us our half time adjustments and before I knew it we were on the field once again.

As we took the field, the crowd was still doing their best to keep us up beat, cheering our every step onto the field. The guys lined up along the sideline but I was off on my own, visualizing the first drive. Under no circumstance, I knew that I could turn the ball over or go without at least making a hell of a drive. And, that is exactly what I did.

We played it conservative at the start of the second half. There was a lot of short passes with a high completion rate but every time we would find ourselves in the end zone they would counter with a touchdown of their own. We went back-and-forth all second half and, in the final minutes of the forth quarter, we both found ourselves tied at 49.

Things were disintegrating for us on our end. Time was not on our side, and St. Michaels had all of the momentum in the world. They had switched it up and started running the ball on us. We could not stop one run. Every time the running back touched the ball he'd gain five yards, then eight yards, then seven, then ten and on and on it went.

Not only were they moving the ball, they were killing the clock too. The clock had dipped below thirty-seconds and St. Michaels was on our thirty-yard line, threatening to score. Because they had run the ball, the time did not stop. There wasn't going to be a chance for our boys to get out there. It was all up to the defense. The only way I was going to touch the football one more time in a Colts uniform, was if we stopped them.

Their kicker warmed up on the sidelines across the field positioned to hit the game winning field goal. From studying the film and scouting report, I knew St. Michael's kicker had one hell of a leg, and was already in field goal position. Everyone knew that St. Michaels was going to run the ball one last time to give their kicker a better shot at winning the game. St. Michaels had one last time out to use, so if they ran it one more time they would be able to melt the clock down to three or four-seconds, giving the kicker the chance to win the game if he made it, or send us into overtime if he missed it. Either way, St. Michaels was in a great position to win the State Championship.

I sat on one knee off to the side of the cluster of our players on the sideline with my helmet praying that the defense would be able to get some penetration through the line and knock their offense back a few yards to make it harder for their kicker to kick the ball through the uprights.

St. Michaels quarterback called the cadence. Nearly everyone on their offensive players was on the line of scrimmage showing an obvious run play. The ball snapped right into the quarterback's hands and he turned to the running back to hand the ball off. I turned to the line of scrimmage hoping someone might have gotten through the line with ease but none did.

And then it happened.

When the quarterback turned to hand the ball off to his running back, he placed the ball at his running back's chest. The ball bounced off of the running back's pads and onto the ground. Because when the running back was moving forward the ball had bounced forward to the back feet of the lineman. The lineman did not see or notice that the ball was on the ground right behind them, giving only the running back who had just fumbled the ball, a chance to recover the ball.

When everyone on the sideline cheering for Hagerman including cadets and football players saw that ball bounced off of their running backs pads onto the ground, I yelled at the top of my lungs, "FUMBLE!" I jumped from my knee and kept on shouting it over and over again. Everyone joined in with me screaming, "Get on the ball!"

A pile up occurred. The offense line realized there was a fumble, the defensive line and linebackers saw the ball hit the ground, and everyone's eyes looked downward for the ball. It took mere moments for everyone to see where the ball had landed and literally every single player in both red and blue jerseys dove in the direction of it. The pile of bodies around the area of where the ball lay happened so fast that at first, I could not see who jumped on it. I shouted at everyone on the sideline, "Can anyone see who jumped on the ball first?"

The officials blew their whistles calling an official timeout to check and see who had possession of the ball. The refs leaped on the pile trying to pull players off of it and see if they could find the ball. I stood in suspense with everyone else desperate to know what was going on inside the pile at that moment. It honestly did not matter who touched the ball first, because now, with no ref being able to see what was going on down at the bottom of the pile, it was about who was the strongest and who would be able to maintain possession long enough for the referees to see.

The crowd was dead silent as the refs pulled off the players one-by-one. All of us prayed that someone had managed to come up with the ball. If we had the ball, we were still alive, but if St. Michaels held onto it, it would give their kicker a shot to win the game, and send us home with a loss.

Referees were still on top of the ball peering through any little gap to see. Suddenly, one of the referees on top of the pile jumped off and pointed in our direction.

"We got it," I said. "We fucking got it."

The Hagerman fans went wild shouting and jumping up and down.

When the pile had come undone, one of our defensive tackles stood holding the football tight in his hands. The defense all jumped on him pumped up. We had needed a big play and holy shit, did we get one. Not a moment too soon.

Coach Lou attempted to settle us down. "Take a knee, Rocky," he said. "Lets take this game into overtime. If we move the ball with twenty-three seconds left on the clock there's a shot at a turnover and we could give them the ball right back on our side of the field."

"You're right." I said and shouted to the offense, "Get back on the field. Let's take this game into overtime."

We lined up and I snapped the ball into my hands and quickly took a knee. I tossed the ball to the ref and me and the other Hagerman captains met their captains at center field along with the refs about to head into overtime.

The referee informed us that we would play an extra ten-minute period to determine who the winner of the State Championship would be. "Okay, men, each team will get the football at their opponents 25 yard line, and each team will have an opportunity to possess the ball. If the game is still tied after the first overtime will go into a second overtime and continue this until a winner is determined. Understand?"

I spoke for the team. "Yes, we get it."

The referee narrowed his eyes at me. "Then call heads or tails, sir."

I looked at Brett who indicated he wanted me to call tails.

"Tails," I shouted out loud.

We won the coin toss and elected to defend to start the overtime. Like in the beginning of the game, we captains shook our opponents hands and returned to our sideline. "We're starting out on defense," I said.

This was the first overtime of the season. My men looked panicked. It was no consolation that the opposing team felt the same way.

The crowd continued to stay on their feet cheering at the top of their voices, as the defense got ready to take the field.

They had a look with hunger in their eyes as they prepared to get out there and hit someone. It made me excited to get my shot to put some points on the board.

St. Michaels took the field and everyone one of us, who watched the defense bolt out there shouted at them, "We need to stop."

In the first play of overtime our defensive tackles busted through the line and sacked the quarterback. A hell of a start, but it did not last that long as the offense again started to move the football.

St. Michaels was running short crossing plays, which allowed for them to easily move the ball. Our defense was more concerned about letting St. Michaels score a touchdown that they were dropping back into a conservative zone coverage, leaving the short routes uncovered. Little-by-little they moved the football until eventually they had crossed their ten yard line and threatened to score.

Standing on the sideline I screamed words of encouragement to our defense. I knew that they had it in them to stop these guys, and hold them to a field goal. If they could just hold them, I could put the ball in the end zone and win the game. First and ten, St. Michaels lined up in a run formation where they ran the ball straight up the gut for a gain of five. That five-yard gain alone was not what we needed. Again, St. Michaels lined up in a run formation and they ran the ball for four yards this time putting it on the one-yard line. It was actually so close that I thought that they had scored a touchdown. When I saw the referees wave their hands over their heads indicating that their running back had come up just short, I exhaled a breath of relief.

Everyone in that stadium thought that there was no way that St. Michaels could not score on third down with less than a yard to go. Everyone but me. I had a feeling down in the pit of my stomach that this defense that had been looked over all season, had something left in the tank, something that would give us a shot to win the game.

St. Michael's quarterback lined up in a run formation again, and we countered stacking everyone in the box, putting them right at the line of scrimmage, anticipating the run straight up the middle.

He snapped the ball and turned to hand the ball off to his running back. But at the last second, he pulled it away and boot legged it around the line of scrimmage. They were running a play action fake with third and one and everyone in the stadium had been totally faked out. Everyone but our outside linebacker. He saw that quarterback pull that ball in at the last second and blitzed right off of the right tackle, with no one there to pick him up. St. Michael's quarterback rolled around with his tight end whom had broke from the line, wide open in the back of the end zone. But right as he looked up, our linebacker was right in his face. He wrapped him up and threw him to the ground, giving their quarterback absolutely zero chance at even getting the ball off.

The only thing that ran through my mind at that moment, with everyone jumping and screaming around me, was oh my God, we can win this game. Then their kicking team ran out onto the field. Because of that sack, pushing them back close to five yards, there was no way St. Michaels would go for it and risk losing important points.

While everyone prepared for the field goal attempt, I gathered my offense on the sideline. They were all still jacked from what had just happened with our defense, but I needed to calm them down and regain their focus. Yes, the defense had put us in a spot to win it twice, but now it was up to us to win this game.

Once they were calm and in a huddle on the sideline, I said as the ball was being kicked, "This is our chance guys. The defense did their job, they have entrusted us to win this. It does not matter at this point who is the strongest. It does not matter who is the fastest. All that matters is how bad you want it. No more coaching, no more practicing. It all comes down to right here and right now." I paused and looked at the ten who had been with me for this incredible journey. I glared into their eyes, as St. Michaels had completed their field goal, and the ball was being lined up at the twenty-five yard line for our chance to score.

And with that, the offense stormed the field as ready as they were ever going to be. I followed behind the offense who had formed up in a shotgun. We all knew the first three plays because Coach Castro had told us what they were going to be, while the defense was out there first.

"It's up to you, Rocky," Coach Castro whispered to me prior to us running on the field. "After the first three plays, you will make the play call. Either way, I want you to run the hurry up offense, and not allow for St. Michaels to switch up there defensive personal."

It was a bold move for the coaching staff to do this, but I could tell that they weren't in it to tie, and send us to a second overtime. They wanted us to win it, and win it right now.

"Go!" I yelled, and the ball was snapped into my hands. I immediately threw it to my right, where Brett had perfectly positioned himself for a screen pass. He managed to pick up six yards before being brought down. We all ran to the line of scrimmage, knowing what the second play was going to be.

"Ready, set, go!" I yelled and the ball was again snapped. I turned to hand it off to Donte, but he was immediately stuffed at the line for a no gain, making it third and four.

"Go!" I called and the ball was snapped. I dropped back three steps and looked down field for Brett, who was running hook pattern. St. Michael's corners were double teaming him, knowing that Brett was my favorite target, giving him no chance at getting open. I looked left at Steven who was running a ten-yard outside flat route, but he too was completely smothered by their corners. Donte started to break from the backfield, but as he was breaking, one of their ends got loose from Borris, and I did not have time to wait for Donte to turn the corner. So, I stepped up into the pocket causing the defense end to miss me. Realizing that the pocket had begun to collapse, I started to break out of it, still behind the line of scrimmage and looking down field to make a throw. At this point, my receivers ran anywhere they could throughout their secondary. But they just weren't able to find the holes. Every option I looked at I thought was just too risky, and could possibly end up in a turnover, which would lose the game for us. So I tucked the ball and started to run. I knew that I didn't have much space to pick up the four yards and there were two linebackers close by.

With two yards to go before the fist down, I covered the ball with both my hands. Both linebackers hit me simultaneously. I kept myself low, and drove my feet as hard as I could into the wall of linebackers. I thought I was going nowhere but had managed to push them back just far enough for half of my body to cross over the first down marker, giving us a brand new set of downs to work with.

When the referee signaled for a first down, I felt beyond relieved, but there was no time to celebrate. I rushed everyone to the 15-yard line while the ref set the ball for the next play.

St. Michael's defense grew more and more tired with every play. Guys were sweating bullets falling down on the field. Their coaches desperately wanted to sub some of their guys out but couldn't without getting flagged for too many men on the field, or worse, without us catching them with their pants down and scoring a touchdown to a wide open receivers whose corner left him for the bench.

I pushed our offense to the line where I made the call, for which play we were going to run. I yelled up and down the field and made sure that everyone knew what we were doing. Moments later, I snapped the ball and both receivers were off and moving. I dropped back and looked down field and again both of my receivers were smothered. Knowing that Arturo was going to break from his block any second I hesitated, and when he broke I tossed the ball right over the line and right into Arturo's hands. He turned up field and was just blasted by a middle linebacker, just waiting for him.

By some miracle, Arturo popped up like it was an average hit, when in reality that was a brutal blow.

Again, we rushed to the line, with me calling the play at the line as people were setting up. St. Michael's corners were looking to the sidelines, almost begging to get a sub in.

"Go!" With the ball in my hands, I dropped back looking in Brett's direction. The corner on top of him had slipped when Brett made his break running a skinny post route. He must have tripped over himself or lost his footing because he was on the ground and Brett was wide open, just yards away from the end zone. Without even analyzing the safeties positions, I cocked the ball back and let it go.

As soon as I released the football, I knew I had made a crucial mistake. The ball was good, a tight one on target with a good spiral, and a lot of velocity behind it. But I had failed to look off one of the safeties and he had broke for the ball the moment he saw my eyes lock onto Brett. He had made such a good break that I thought for sure he would be right in front of Brett as the ball reached its target to intercept it and end the game. He held his hands up and the ball landed into the safeties hands and then bounced right out of them.

My hands went onto my helmet, as I released the football.

But when St. Michael's safety dropped it, I crouched down over my knees, knowing that I had just dodged a bullet and prevented history from repeating itself. While I looked down feeling sorry for myself at what I had nearly done, I saw the secondary trying to run off of the field to substitute out.

No one else on the offense recognized this except for me. Seeing that St. Michaels was taking such a big risk to get fresh legs onto the field I yelled for everyone to the ball.

In those few seconds, it was total chaos. My offense did not really know what was going on, but my men trusted me and did as I said. The defense, knowing we were trying to slip a fast one on them was sprinting to their positions. While everyone lined up I called the play at the line of scrimmage. Still, there was total confusion on both sides of the field. The defense really did not know where to line up and a lot of my guys hadn't even heard the play.

But I didn't care. I knew I could take advantage of what was going on.

Opposite me, the defensive linebacker called the defensive play to his guys, based on what we were doing. I stepped back into a shotgun formation. I then looked forward at Archie with people still on their defense running around. With us set, I snapped the ball into my hands then faked the handoff to Donte. Then, I took a step back to look over my receivers. There was some hesitation at first because at the bullet I had just dodged, but once the ball had touched my hands, it was like that near interception never happened. I stood tall in the pocket ready to make a throw. Moments later, I looked down the field as the pocket began to collapse.

I had all of my eligible receivers including Donte and Arturo down field in the end zone and I knew that I could win it right then. I stepped up into the pocket to try and buy me some more time but that did little to help.

One blitzing linebacker managed to bull rush one of the Sanford brothers back and grab a handful of my jersey as he fell down. I shoved his hand off of me making me clear of a sack by him.

I had less than a second to make a decision or else this pocket would fall apart and I'd have to take the sack. At the last moment, I broke from the pocket running in between my blockers and the defense to the right side of the field that had more space to move. I succeeded in getting over to the right side of the field looking down field. There was no one open in the end zone. If I tried to throw that ball to any one of my guys, it would for sure be picked off. The only shot I had to score was to buy some more time in the backfield. If I tried to tuck the ball and run, I wouldn't make it very far. There were two linebackers a couple of yards in front of the goal line, eyeing me and watching for the run. If I tried to take off, I would maybe get six yards before being brought down, and that wouldn't even get us a first down, much less the touchdown.

Standing there looking around, I felt panic in the pit of stomach and thought the smart thing to do was to throw the ball away, wasting our third down, and let our kicker come out and tie the game for us. This would force us into a second overtime. But I didn't want that. I didn't want to risk us blowing this opportunity to take a chance to find another one to win the game later. We needed to win now!

I had reached the sideline, on the right side of the field, and there was no more room for me to go. To the left, those rushing me were still being blocked but we were starting to get loose from my lineman. If I could get to the opposite end of the field behind the line of scrimmage, there would be a line of blockers who had just been beaten waiting there for me to buy me more time. I waited for the last possible moment realizing that no one was open before I made my move to get to the opposite end.

I dodged defensive players left and right and managed to get halfway through the mess going on behind the line of scrimmage. Then, one of the defense players managed to get a hand on my foot as he went down, and made me lose my balance. I lunged forward with the ball in my left hand, and put my right hand on the ground in an attempt to regain balance. While I fell forward, I put my right hand in front of me and pushed off of the ground with all that I had and miraculously regained my balance.

I stood tall again and peered down the field. Arturo had found a small gap in the secondary big enough for me to get the ball through. I would have to make it into one hell of a gap. The blitzing linebacker who had gotten a hold of my jersey earlier, barreled down on me. There was no one there to stop him. He was going to hit me, full steam, regardless if I made the throw or not. With no time to spare, I decided I was going to determine the outcome of this game, no one else, just me.

I opened my shoulders giving me the best possible position to make an accurate throw and also provide the linebacker an easy target to hit. I brought the ball back and threw it with everything I had. There was little room for error. As the ball left my hand, I was thrown down hard to the ground, as the defensive linebacker had left his feet and speared the crown of his helmet straight into my chest.

At that point, everything went dark. The linebacker was on top of me and I could not see a thing. I heard a monstrous scream arise from the crowed. Because of the screaming, I knew something major had just happened. Either we had just caught the ball and scored the game's winning touchdown, or the defense had intercepted the ball and we just lost the State Championship.

I finally scrambled out from underneath the linebacker before my whole offensive line tackled me again. They shouted and screamed and tears ran down some of their faces.

I had just made the throw of my life and we had won the state championship. I stood up from my lineman tackle. Arturo stood in the back of the end zone holding the ball with the entire football team surrounding him.

I ran toward my guys to celebrate with my brothers. I had waited so long for this moment dreaming and praying to get another chance to come back here and win the big game. I jumped through the pile of celebrating Colts totally mugged by everyone there. I can't describe what we all felt in that moment. We had worked so hard through all of the unique stresses of military school managing to have the strength to put together a remarkable, magical run. The championship was not just for this team, but also for everyone wearing a uniform at Hagerman Military Institute.

The celebration carried on the field for a long time. A lot of the guys had family members on the field congratulating them. I celebrated with Brogan, Beal, Brett and Karen. It was an awesome feeling to finally get over the hump and win a championship. I was overcome with emotion and felt a joy inside that was indescribable.

The team eventually made their way to the locker room where guys were still overcome with excitement. I hugged each and every one of them and thanked them for sticking behind me. When I reached my last teammate, Coach Lou came up from behind me and held at his hand to shake. A hug would have been way too much to ask from the man. "You proved a lot of people wrong tonight, including myself."

"I'm just glad I could win this for us all," I said smiling.

"I'm very proud of you, Rocky. I want you to stick and celebrate with the guys but there is actually a college scout in the hall. He says he wants to talk to you."

"Now?"

"Yeah, he was pretty adamant about meeting you tonight."

"Sure, okay," I said. "Give me a minute and I'll be out there."

I turned and took my shoulder pads off and put them in my locker along with my helmet and made my way out of the locker room and headed down the hall where I could see to a man leaning on the wall dressed in a rather shabby grey pinstriped suit.

He didn't look like any of the other recruits I had met when I played for Premium. I extended my hand. "Hello, sir, I'm Rocky."

The man had a bushy mustache and a sadness in his eyes. "Hello, Rocky. It's my great pleasure to meet you. A hell of a game you played tonight."

He had a slight Spanish accent. "Thank you. It was really a

team effort. I couldn't have done it without my guys."

"You're modest, kid." The man fixed his tie and looked off behind me as if to check if someone would interrupt our conversation.

"Coach Lou told me you wanted to speak with me."

He smiled. "Yeah, I have been wanting to speak with you for a while."

"Really? What school are you from, sir?"

"I'm ah, not from a school."

"What do you mean? You are a scout aren't you?"

The man looked behind me again. "No, I'm not a scout."

"Than who the hell are you?" For some reason, this man freaked me out.

"I'm your father."

CHAPTER NINETEEN

Bullshit." I said taking a step backwards.

"It's true, my name is Diego Montoya, and I am your father. I lied to your coach to be able to get in to the locker room to speak with you."

I didn't know what to feel. I was extremely skeptical of this stranger who stood there lying to my face. There was something about this man that made me uncomfortable. I started to walk away. "Don't follow me."

Diego pulled out his wallet from his back pocket and took out something from inside of it. "I have something that can prove what I am saying is true."

"What kind of proof?" I asked, turning to face him.

He handed me an old crumpled up picture. The man in the photo had a full beard, and was a lot skinnier back then, but it was the man standing in front of me. A woman who looked like a younger version of my mother stood next to him with an infant in her arms. I had seen the same picture before in my mom's room.

"So you believe me now?" he said studying my face.

A part of me wanted to punch the guy in the face, while

another part of me just wanted to walk away and pretend that none of this had happened. "Okay. Maybe you are who you say you are. But what the hell difference does it make?"

"I want to get to know you, son. Can you meet me tomorrow at the Starbucks across the street from the stadium?"

I hesitated for a minute thinking what to say. "I guess I could slip away."

"Excellent," he said and turned away from me in an awkward fashion.

As I headed back toward the locker room, I didn't know why I so easily agreed to meeting up with him. I was more curious than anything else. What did this man, my father have to say to me after all these years?

I returned to the locker room to celebrate with my teammates but my heart was no longer into it. Instead I was consumed with this stranger who had just barreled into my life unexpectedly. Thoughts swirled through my mind. I was so confused and didn't want to tell anyone what had just happened.

As I lay in bed that night, I didn't know what to do. Should I give this stranger a second chance or should I just tell him off and be done with him? But I desperately wanted to know why he abandoned me as a child. I had spent years imagining what a meeting like this would be like. All the questions I might ask my father if he'd come back into my life. Then a thought popped into my head. What if the guy just wanted to get to know me because he had read about me in the paper? There was a lot of media attention about me, and the Hagerman team in all the New Mexico papers. Brett's parents had cut out articles from the sports section of the Albuquerque Journal and he'd pasted them in a scrapbook. What if this man had just read about me and thought being the father of the State Champion quarterback would get him something? It had been eighteen years and suddenly the guy finally shows up, moments after I had been the star quarterback in the New Mexico State Championship.

I tossed and turned all night before I came to a decision on what I needed to know and what I was going to do. When the next morning came, I woke up early enough to sneak out of the hotel and get to Starbucks.

Diego was already seated at a table reading a newspaper. I sat down face-to-face with him. He put the paper down and smiled at me. "Hello, Rocky."

"Hi," I said, thinking what a huge mistake I had just made.

"Do you want any coffee?"

"I'm fine."

"It's been a long time," he said.

"I wouldn't know. You're just a stranger to me."

He reached out and touched my hand. "I want to be more than a stranger."

"Okay," I said withdrawing my hand. "What is it you do with yourself after eighteen years?"

"I work for a construction company now. I am married and have two children. Both are in their mid-teens," he said proudly. He pulled out his iPhone and shuffled screens to find some pictures of his boys and handed me the phone.

I shoved his phone back across the table not interested in looking at photos of his sons. They were my half-brothers but I didn't want to look at their pictures. All I felt was he'd insulted my existence. "So you pretty much got a family do-over."

"No, that's not it at all. I just needed a change, that's all."

"A change?"

"Yeah, you know, things just weren't working out so I needed a change. You get it, don't you?"

"Get what? The fact that my father lost interest in me and took off? No, I don't get that. That's something a coward would do. You ran away from your problems turning a blind eye to the people you hurt. Me, for one."

"I'm sorry if I hurt you, I just thought it best."

"How is being raised without a father in my best interest? Can you honestly sit here, look me in the eye, and say that?" It blew me away that these words were coming out of my mouth. Words I had wanted to say for years.

"If you were in my position you would have done the same thing," he said.

He honestly believed he'd done the right thing? At least that's what he'd told himself so he could sleep at night. "I hope if I was in that position I would never even consider doing what you did to me. Why even contact me? Why now?"

"I just felt the time was right."

"I bet you did," I said sarcastically. It was clear to me the real reason he was there. He just wanted to be associated with a State Champion. The piece of shit was so convinced that he had made the right call that it sickened me. My frustration grew into anger and I wanted to get the hell out of there.

I supposed the old Rocky would have simply walked away or probably worse. He might have even popped the guy square in the jaw. But that wasn't me anymore. I was a changed man.

"Do you not want me in your life?" the stranger said blinking his eyes a little too fast.

"Do you really want to know what I want?"

"I do," he said.

I sat up straight and looked him dead in the eye. "I am furious at you, Diego Montoya. You have done terrible things that you will never realize. You are the reason why my mother has so many problems. She has suffered from the loss of you and struggled just to keep a roof over our heads and food on the table. But not only that, not having a father growing up is something that no boy should have to deal with. And you did that to me."

"I don't know what to say," he interrupted.

"Just be quiet and listen to me. For as long as I can remember, I have always asked why my father left me. But I realized it did not matter why. All that mattered was the fact that he left and that was something I was going to have to deal with growing up. And I have until now. I have hated you every single day of my life until right now. There is only one reason why I wanted to sit in front of you today and that is to say one thing: I forgive you."

"Excuse me?"

"Do you know how exhausting it is to hate someone every day. It tears you up inside. But worst of all it gives you all the power over me. Honestly, you don't deserve one drop of power over me. I have done more than most with what I started with, and I am proud to say that I did it. But I am done hating you and I am done asking questions about you. Hell, I am just done with you. I appreciate you coming down to meet me but this is where our relationship ends."

With that, I stood up and moved toward the door. He didn't even try to stop me. His face was red as I left him there. With every step I took, I grew more confident that what I said was the right thing for me to do. I could feel it, surfacing through the shakiness, a growing sense of peace. I breathed more deeply.

For my whole life I'd never acted in my best interest until that very morning, and now I knew what it felt like to face my fears head on. As I pushed the glass door open, it dawned on me that this was the lesson that Hagerman had taught me. Sometimes a man needs to make a tough decision for himself. The right decision at the right moment. Life is about the decisions we make, both small and big. I knew I needed to make this one and not look back.

ACKNOWLEDGMENTS

Many thanks to my parents Anthony Reeve and Jacquelyn Montoya for their belief in me.

Special thanks to Karen Leigh and Lexy Martinez for helping me to initially edit the book.

Cover Design: Anna K. Sargent

Developmental Editing: Lara Reznik

Proof Editing: Mari Anixter

Interior Design: Tosh McIntosh

Tony Reeve grew up in Albuquerque, New Mexico. He attended the New Mexico Military Institute (NMMI) in Roswell. He says that the experience at military school was the most trying and difficult time of his life but it helped him to develop into the person he is today. It was also a time filled with incredible stories and everlasting friendships.

After Tony graduated from NMMI, he attended DePaul University in Chicago, Illinois, majoring in accounting and minoring in finance. Yes, that's correct, an accountant who writes fictional stories. He received his BA in 2013, and is currently pursuing an MBA in Southern California. When he is not studying for the CPA or his MBA, Tony enjoys participating in adult flag football, ice hockey, and Crossfit. One day he would like to own a multitude of businesses while continuing a career as an author.

Connect with Tony online:
Email: tony109649@hotmail.com
Twitter: @tony109649
Instagram: tonyreeve22
Facebook: www.facebook.com/tony.reeve

18457150R00145